Space Trivia

William R. Pogue

All rights reserved under article two of the Berne Copyright Convention (1971).
No part of this book may be reproduced or transmitted in any form or by any means,
electronic or mechanical, including photocopying, recording, or by any information storage
and retrieval system without permission in writing from the publisher.
We acknowledge the financial support of the Government of Canada through
the Book Publishing Industry Development Program for our publishing activities.
Published by Apogee Books an imprint of Collector's Guide Publishing Inc.
Box 62034, Burlington, Ontario, Canada, L7R 4K2
Printed and bound in Canada
Space Trivia
by William R. Pogue
contributing editor Robert Godwin
cover design Ryan G. Smith
ISBN 1-896522-98-X
Copyright © 2003 Apogee Books / William R. Pogue
All photos courtesy of NASA

Space Trivia

William R. Pogue

contributing editor

Robert Godwin

Space Trivia – Questions 1 to 800

1. What was the first living creature to orbit the Earth in a man-made spacecraft?

A Russian dog named Laika, aboard Sputnik 2, Nov 3, 1957. *See Q 407.*

InfoNote: Laika is Russian for "Barker" or "Husky" and it is also the name of a breed of small dogs. Her name had been Kudryavka (Little Curly) until just before flight. It has never been clear why her name was changed. When the Russians were too slow to release the name of the dog (Laika) the media gave her the temporary name, Mutnik.

2. What booster rocket was used to launch John Glenn into orbit in 1962?

A modified Atlas, a U. S. Air Force Intercontinental Ballistic Missile (ICBM).

3. How many U.S. crews landed on the Moon during the Apollo program?

Six two-man crews landed on the Moon. Apollo missions 11, 12, 14, 15, 16 and 17.

4. What is the largest living organism visible from Earth orbit?

The Great Barrier Reef. (It lies off the NE coast of Australia and is living coral.)

5. Which astronaut served as U.S. ambassador to Norway after leaving NASA?

William A. (Bill) Anders (Apollo 8). He was ambassador to Norway from 1976-77.

6. What is used as a reflective coating on the space suit helmet visor?

Gold.

7. Who discovered the Earth's radiation belts?

Dr. James van Allen, University of Iowa physicist, using data from Explorer 1 (1958). *See Q 635.*

8. Who is the only astronaut who made space flights on all five of the Shuttles?

Story Musgrave.

9. Which two planetariums were used to train astronauts for the Apollo program?

The Morehead Planetarium (University of North Carolina) and the Griffith Observatory planetarium, Los Angeles, California.

10. What organization adopted the first rules to govern the award of official records for space flights?

The Fédération Aéronautique Internationale (FAI), at Barcelona, Spain on October 7, 1960.

11. Who was the only astronaut to fly in Mercury, Gemini and Apollo spacecraft?

Walter M. (Wally) Schirra, Jr. He flew on Mercury 8, Gemini 6, and Apollo 7.

12. Which Shuttle never made it into orbit?

The Enterprise. It was used for the Approach and Landing Test program in 1977. *See Q 227, 333.* The Enterprise is now at the Dulles facility of the Smithsonian Air and Space Museum.

13. Who launched the first liquid propellant rocket?

Dr. Robert H. Goddard (March 16, 1926) at Auburn, Massachusetts.

14. Who were the first mice to encounter weightlessness?

Amy, Sally and Moe (October 13, 1960, aboard an Atlas rocket for 20 minutes of zero-g).

15. How many orbits did John Glenn make on his first space flight?

Three.

16. Who was the first paying passenger on a space flight?

Toyohiro Akiyama, a Japanese journalist sponsored by his television network (for $10 million). He spent a week aboard the Russian Mir space station in December 1990.

17. In what building at the Cape Canaveral Air Force Station, were the Mercury astronauts' crew quarters located?

Hangar S.

18. What was the first American space mission to make an emergency return from space?

Titles for Spacefarers

The terms, astronaut and cosmonaut are synonymous and are used for people who have been selected to train to fly in space or who have flown in space. It just so happened that the U. S. chose the term, astronaut (although the term, cosmonaut, was considered) and the Russians chose the term, cosmonaut to describe the profession of space travelers. NASA breaks down the astronaut crew title into three other categories: Pilot (& Commander), Mission Specialist and Payload Specialist.

Pilot/Commander (Plt/Cdr): A career astronaut selected by NASA to serve as Pilot and (later) Commander of the Shuttle.

Mission Specialist (MS): A career astronaut selected by NASA to perform technical/scientific work and operational tasks such as space walks and operation of the robot arm (RMS or SRMS). See Q 213.

Payload Specialist (PS): An astronaut selected by a non-NASA sponsor to fly a space mission because of outstanding knowledge or skill related to a specific discipline, instrument or facility provided by the sponsor. A PS may also be selected because of political status or to enhance U. S. diplomatic ties. (See Q 22, 191). The PS does not compete in a NASA astronaut selection but is trained to have a safe level of knowledge of Shuttle systems and operations. Normally a PS makes only one flight into space. However, one PS made three Shuttle flights. See Q. 327.

Guest Cosmonaut (GC): The Russian's GC designation is similar to our PS.

Gemini 8. An attitude control rocket stuck "ON", causing the spacecraft to tumble wildly. Neil Armstrong and Dave Scott disabled the primary attitude rockets by pulling circuit breakers and activated the reentry attitude rockets to stop the tumble. The situation forced them to make a premature return to Earth.

19. Who was the first non-NASA astronaut to fly in space on the Shuttle?

Actually, there were two. Byron Lichtenberg (U.S.) and Wulf Merbold (Netherlands) flew as Payload Specialists on the first launch of the European-built Spacelab (Columbia, STS-9, November 1983). See sidebar, **Titles for Spacefarers**.

20. How many space flights are each of the Shuttles designed to make?

100 flights.

21. Which U.S. program was the first to provide private radio calls for astronauts and their families?

Skylab. Every third day a 4-6 minute call was arranged.

22. Who was the first in-office politician to fly in space?

U.S. Senator, Jake Garn (Utah) flew aboard Shuttle mission 51D in April 1985.

23. Who was the first woman to be awarded the Congressional Space Medal of Honor?

Shuttle Mission Specialist Shannon W. Lucid. She was cited for "extraordinary service to the nation" which encompassed five Shuttle missions and a 188-day stay aboard the Mir space station.

24. Who was the first person to do a space walk from a U.S. spacecraft?

Edward H. (Ed) White II, Gemini 4, June 1965.

25. When was the first 3-man crew launched into space?

October 12, 1964. Cosmonauts Komarov, Feoktistov and Yegorov aboard Voskhod 1.

26. Shuttle missions are now designated as STS-88, for example. What does STS stand for?

Space Transportation System.

27. What color is the sky in space (looking away from the Earth)?

Black.

28. Who was the first American to go into space (above 50 miles)?

Alan B. (Al) Shepard, Jr., on Mercury 3 (May 5, 1961). Robert M. (Bob) White was the first X-15 pilot to fly into space (July 17, 1962).

29. What are the names of the five Shuttles that have flown in space?

Columbia, Challenger, Discovery, Atlantis and Endeavour.

30. What is the name of the Japanese winged space vehicle designed for space flight research?

HOPE.

31. What was the name of the disintegrated comet that collided with the planet Jupiter in 1995?

Shoemaker-Levy 9, (If you said Shoemaker or Levy count it correct.) *See Q 134.*

32. Which Shuttle astronaut was born in China?

Shannon W. Lucid, born January 14, 1943 in Shanghai.

33. How much weight does a typical astronaut lose during the first three days in space?

About three pounds (Earth equivalent), due principally to fluid (water) loss. On Skylab a Body Mass Measurement Device (BMMD) was first used to determine body mass (or weight).

34. Why will a space suit, custom tailored on Earth, fit too tight in weightlessness?

People become taller in space. *See sidebar,* **Space Stretch**.

Space Stretch

In zero-g or weightlessness a person's spine will lengthen 1.5 to 2 inches making them 3% taller. This causes a tight fit around the shoulders if allowances aren't provided. This increase in body length was first documented on Skylab 4 (1973), when we made the first complete set of body measurements. The spinal lengthening occurs because the discs between the vertebrae expand in the absence of compression load or weight. Height or body length returns to normal after the space flight. On Earth a similar but not as pronounced effect occurs during a full night's sleep (the overnight stretch is approximately ½ inch).

35. What is the name of the British scientist who formulated the theory of gravitation?

Sir Isaac Newton (1643-1727).

36. Which Earth-launched satellite was the first to leave our solar system?

Pioneer 10. It was launched in March 1972 and, on 13 June 1983 it crossed the orbit of Pluto, the outermost planet known to exist in the solar system. See Q 637, 767.

InfoNote: Pioneer 10 was also the first satellite to cross the asteroid belt. See Q 455. NASA maintained contact with Pioneer 10 until January 22, 2003 (31 years) at which time it was over 7 ½ billion miles (12 billion kilometers) from the Sun. This is roughly twice the distance from the Sun to Pluto. Pluto's average distance from the Sun is approximately 3 ½ billion miles (6 billon kilometers).

Neat Quote: "It remains only to perform certain necessary preliminary experiments before an apparatus can be constructed that will carry recording instruments to any desired altitude." Dr. Robert H. Goddard, 1920.

37. What is the White Room?

The White Room is a room on the Rotating Service Structure (RSS) and provides entry to the Shuttle spacecraft. It has special entrances and stringent rules to prevent contamination of the spacecraft. See Q 83 sidebar, and Q 202, 468, 700.

38. Where is the control center for all NASA planetary and deep space probes?

At NASA's Jet Propulsion Laboratory, Pasadena, California.

39. Apollo astronauts trained for Moon landings using the LLTV. What does LLTV stand for?

Lunar Landing Training Vehicle. The LLTV, built by Bell Aerospace, was dubbed the "flying bedstead" or "pipe rack" and was powered by jet and rocket engines.

Photo of Lunar Landing Training Vehicle (flying bedstead).

40. What piece of aircraft flight gear was used as a model for the astronauts' Snoopy Cap?

The British Royal Air Force (RAF) cloth helmet (circa 1968).

InfoNote: In November 1968, Jim Lovell of the Apollo 8 crew reported an irritating problem with the lightweight headsets developed for Apollo. They were so light that when moving around the cabin of the Command Module the cable from the Intercom box tended to snag on structure and rip the headset off. He asked if anyone had an idea. I told him about the RAF cloth helmet and Jim asked if I could get him one.
I called Mavis Lear a friend I had flown with while on exchange with the RAF. She sent me a helmet immediately by express delivery and Jim gave it to the NASA people to use as a model for what became known as the "Snoopy Cap." Jim was so grateful that he sent Mavis a picture of the first "Earthrise" photographed from the Moon, signed by Frank Borman, Bill Anders and Jim.

John Young wearing Snoopy Cap. See Q 40.

41. To what ambient (space vacuum) temperature extremes are astronauts exposed while on space walks in Earth orbit?

The temperature ranges from -250° F (-150° C) in the dark to +250° F (120° C) in direct sunlight.

42. Which Apollo astronaut landed on the Moon twice?

None did! (Sorry 'bout that.).

43. On what planet will astronaut explorers have to cope with dust storms?

Mars. The winds on Mars can whip up to over 100 miles per hour.

44. Who was the first married couple to fly on the same space crew?

Astronauts Mark C. Lee and Jan N. Davis. They were married during their training for Shuttle mission STS-47 and worked different shifts during their 8-day Spacelab mission (12-20 September 1992).

45. Who wrote the first poem sent into space?

Thomas Burger. The poem, "Space Prober" was placed aboard the Traac satellite. (November 15, 1961).

46. Who was the first person to release a satellite from a spacecraft?

Astronaut Gordon Cooper (Mercury 9-Faith 7, May 1963). Gordo released a 6" sphere that had a strobe light beacon for a visual tracking test.

47. For whom is the Johnson Space Center (JSC) named?

Lyndon B. Johnson, 36th president of the U.S.

48. What officer in charge of rocket sled tests (in the 1950s) served as the test subject?

USAF Colonel John P. Stapp. He rode a sled at 635 m.p.h. (1,017 km per hour) in 1955.

49. Which spacecraft had the first "sit-on" toilet?

Skylab. It had a seat belt to hold you down and a "rear view" mirror to check for spills.

50. What were the first living creatures recovered from Earth orbit?

Two dogs named Strelka (Little Arrow) and Belka (Squirrel) aboard the Sputnik 5 recovery module (April 20, 1960). Rats, mice, flies, plants, fungi and seeds, accompanied them.

51. What does the term TAL site refer to?

Transatlantic Abort Landing site: These are airports especially outfitted to accommodate a Shuttle landing, if a problem occurs during launch. See Q 521.

52. Which crew suggested the nickname "Humpty Dumpty" for their launch booster rocket?

Skylab 4 (third crew). See sidebar, **The Last Laugh.**

53. What organization has first claim to all U.S. space-flown artifacts, excluding personal property of astronauts?

The Smithsonian Institution.

54. What was the first mission directed by the Mission Control Center (MCC) at Houston?

Gemini 4, June, 1965. Previously, control was directed from a concrete blockhouse at Cape Canaveral Air Force Station, Florida.

55. What does NASDA stand for?

The National Space Development Agency of Japan (Japan's counterpart to NASA).

The Last Laugh

Numerous cracks were discovered in the fins of our Skylab 4 booster, delaying launch. Then other cracks were discovered in the truss-work connecting the stages. After the fins were replaced (and the other cracks declared non-hazardous), we suggested (as a gag) the name, "Humpty Dumpty" for the Saturn I B booster. The launch pad crew didn't think it was very funny. They got even the next day and had the last laugh. Just before launch they sent a message that read, "To the crew of Skylab 4, good luck and Godspeed, signed, all the king's horses and all the king's men."

56. What is the name of the Russian launch center for manned space flights?

Baikonur Cosmodrome.

57. In the 20th century which astronaut had to wait the longest to get a space flight?

Don L. Lind. Don was selected in April 1966 and flew on Shuttle mission 51B in April 1985, a patient wait of 19 years.

58. How does a person qualify to join the Association of Space Explorers?

Under current rules, any person who has made one complete orbit of the Earth can join.

59. Which satellite relayed the opening of the 1964 Tokyo Olympics?

Syncom 3. August 19, 1964.

60. Who was the first astronaut to broadcast a live message to radio and TV listeners below?

Wally Schirra, Mercury 8, Sigma 7, October 1962.

61. What is the "X Prize"?

A prize of $10 million. It goes to the first private organization to fly to 100 kilometers (62 miles) altitude with a pilot and two passengers (or equivalent), return to Earth safely and repeat the feat within two weeks. The spacecraft must be privately financed and designed. The prize is offered by the X Prize organization in St. Louis, Missouri.

62. Are Russian spacecraft capable of landing on water?

Yes. However, they greatly prefer a land recovery because a water (sea or ocean) recovery requires such a large area for their recovery forces to accommodate. See Q 287.

63. What is the name of the first element that was launched to begin assembly of the International Space Station (ISS)?

Zarya, meaning Dawn (or Sunrise). It is also referred to as the FGB (Functional Cargo Block) and Control Module. It was built in Russia (paid for by the U. S.) and launched in November 1999 from the Baikonur Cosmodrome.

64. Astronaut Gordon Cooper flew the final Mercury mission. What was his nickname?

Gordo. He had to backup the automatic control system due to an electrical short circuit and he controlled the spacecraft attitude manually for retrofire and reentry. Incidentally,

Gordo was the last astronaut to fly an entire space mission solo.

Neat Quote: *In responding to critics who questioned the need for human crewmembers, a NASA manager responded, "… the success of the mission may well depend upon the actions of the pilot: either in his performance of primary functions or backup functions."*
Dr. George Low, 1959.

65. The large water tank at the Johnson Space Center, Houston (used to train crews for space walks) is named for whom?

Sonny Carter (Manley L. Carter, Jr.), Shuttle astronaut on STS-33. Astronaut Carter died in the crash of a commercial airliner on April 5, 1991.

66. Before Shuttle, which manned program launched the most spacecraft in the shortest time?

Gemini. Ten manned missions in 20 months.

67. Which crew built a Christmas tree from onboard hardware scraps?

The Skylab 4 crew. In December 1973, Jerry Carr, Ed Gibson and I assembled used food cans for the trunk/stem of the tree and attached various metal parts for the limbs and ornaments, including an aluminum foil comet that Ed made for a tree topper (to symbolize our investigation of the Comet Kohoutek). *See Q 306 sidebar.*

68. Who was the first person to fly into space in both Russian and American spacecraft?

Russian Cosmonaut/Astronaut Sergei Krikalev. He flew on Soyuz TM-7 [November 1988]; Soyuz TM-12 [May 1991], STS-60 [January 1994] and STS-88 [December 1998]. In November 2000 he was a member of the first crew to operate the International Space Station.

69. Which space traveler carried the first letter into space?

Cosmonaut Yuri Gagarin. He carried a letter for Cosmonaut Physician V.V. Parin (which Parin had written to his wife, but addressed to himself). The cover of this letter is displayed in a Russian museum.

70. What is the meaning of the NASA initials, "PPK"?

It stands for Personal Preference Kit and is a small bag containing personal artifacts/mementos that astronauts are permitted to carry on space flights.

71. What life form jeopardized the Hubble Space Telescope (HST) while it was in the Shuttle payload bay awaiting launch?

Insects. Mosquitoes, wasps and moths were a constant threat to contaminate the 94-inch mirror of the HST.

72. What is the official language for all aspects of the International Space Station?

English.

73. Who invented the rocket?

The Chinese (invention credited to Feng Jishen, 970 AD). The first written account (1232 AD), describes military uses (to frighten the enemy).

74. What was the name of the first chimpanzee to orbit the Earth?

Enos. He made two orbits on November 29, 1961 in the final Mercury-Atlas orbital test prior to manned flights.

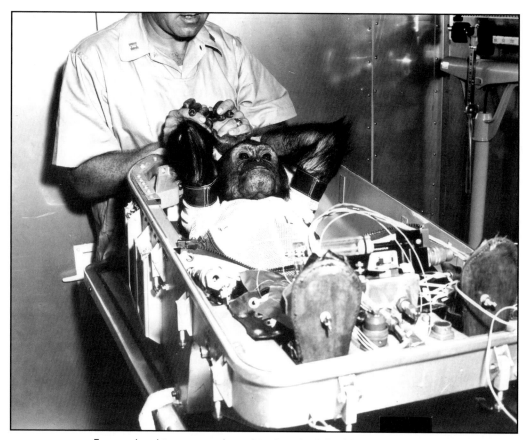

Enos – the chimpanzee who orbited in the Atlas-Mercury mission.

75. As compared to their appearance from Earth how do stars appear when viewed from space?

They don't twinkle and are a bit brighter.

76. What booster rocket was used to launch Gemini spacecraft?

Titan II, modified from an air force ICBM.

77. How long was the umbilical (suit hose) for the first U.S. space-walk (Ed White, Gemini 4)?

25 feet.

78. Which astronauts made two journeys to the Moon (name one)?

Jim Lovell, (Apollo 8 and 13), John Young (Apollo 10 and 16) and Gene Cernan (Apollo 10 and 17).

Crazy Quote: *"This foolish idea of shooting at the Moon is an example of the absurd length to which vicious specialization will carry scientists. To escape the Earth's gravitation a projectile needs a velocity of 7 miles per second. The thermal energy at this speed is 15,180 calories. Hence, the proposition appears to be basically impossible."* Professor W. Bickerton, 1926.

79. Who was the first American woman to do a space-walk (perform extravehicular activity or EVA)?

Kathryn D. (Kathy) Sullivan, Shuttle Mission 41G, October, 1984.

80. What aircraft do the Shuttle astronauts use to train for Shuttle approaches and landings?

The STA (Shuttle Training Aircraft), a heavily modified twin jet Grumman Gulfstream II.

81. The mouth of what major river is located at the Earth's equator?

The Amazon river of Brazil.

82. What is an ASCAN?

ASCAN is an abbreviation for AStronaut CANdidate, their classification after selection. After their first year of successful training ASCANs are then designated astronauts.

83. What astronauts had the title STONEY during the Gemini and Apollo programs?

The astronauts assigned to the launch control team in Florida. *See sidebar,* **Countdown**.

84. What aircraft do astronauts use for flying proficiency and transportation to other NASA work locations?

Countdown

The term, STONEY, came from one of the Mercury launch engineers named Bill Stone but later became a title. Later in the Apollo program, STONEY checked out all the pad safety provisions for the crew and, just before launch, controlled the elevator(s) that the crew rode up to the White Room level before boarding the spacecraft. STONEY also gave the crew a personal countdown to ignition.

I was STONEY for the Apollo 11 launch. Neil Armstrong instructed me, "I don't want you to call ignition 'til you see the fire" (instead of making the call based on the predicted time of ignition). A view of the engines was relayed to a TV screen on my console from a television camera below and to the side of the engines. The camera lasted just long enough to give me a good view of the engines as they lit up and before the video camera was incinerated. See Q 37, 202, 468

The Norair (Northrop) T-38 Talon, a jet trainer. Non-pilot astronauts are trained to fly as second crewmembers and frequently accompany pilots on trips necessary for their work.

85. When exposed to zero-g how much will an average person's waist measurement decrease?

Approximately three inches (7.5 centimeters).

86. Which astronaut became president of Eastern Airlines?

Frank F. Borman II (Gemini 7 and Apollo 8).

87. What NASA insignia was known as the "WORM"?

This is the crawling graphic that spells out the letters NASA. The worm was disliked by many within NASA including a lot of astronauts and, in 1992, was replaced by an earlier NASA design called the Vector logo. The Vector logo was derived from an earlier similar design called the Meatball. In fact, many still refer to the Vector logo as the Meatball. Their general appearance is the same.

88. What was the name of the Soviet chief space designer in the 1950s and 60s?

Sergei P. Korolev.

InfoNote: Chief Designer Korolev's identity was a closely held state secret because the Soviet leaders were afraid he would be targeted for assassination if the West found out who was leading the Russian space effort. His identity was revealed only after he died in January 1966.

89. What was the original name of the Johnson Space Center, Houston, Texas, where the astronauts are based?

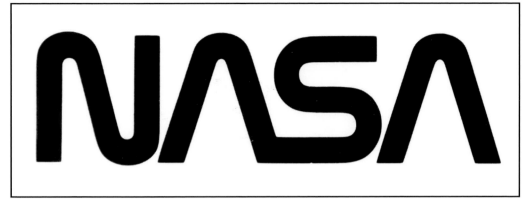

Photo of the Worm. *See Q 87.*

The Manned Spacecraft Center (MSC).

90. What was the name of the secret project that brought Dr. Wernher von Braun and his rocket design team to the U.S. after World War II?

Operation Paperclip.

91. Who conceived and implemented the first Space Camp?

Mr. Edward Buckbee. Now called the U.S. Space Camp, first located in Huntsville, AL.

92. What drag device was added to the Shuttles to decrease the landing roll-out distance?

Drag chutes. First use by the Shuttle was in 1992.

93. To date (January 2003) how many astronauts have been elected to the U.S. Senate?

Two, John H. Glenn, Jr. (Ohio) and Harrison H. (Jack) Schmitt (New Mexico).

94. Which astronaut died during a climb of Mt. Everest?

Dr. Karl Henize, on October 5, 1993. Shuttle astronaut Henize flew aboard mission 51-F (July 1985). *See Q 377.*

95. How many pieces of man-made space debris are orbiting around the Earth?

Over 8,000 pieces larger than a baseball and millions of tiny pieces. *See Table 1,* **Litterbugs**.

96. Who contributed most of the land where the Johnson Space Center (JSC) was built?

Litterbugs			
Size	Number of Objects	% of Total Mass	% of Total Number
greater than 10 cm (4")	8,000	99.93%	0.02%
1 – 10 cm (0.04 "– 4.0")	110,000	0.035%	0.31%
0.1 – 1 cm (0.04" – 0.4")	35,000,000	0.035%	99.67%
Total	35,118,000	100% (200 tons)	100%
Table 1			

Rice University, Houston, Texas (from a tract donated to Rice by the Humble Oil Company).

97. Which astronaut of the 20th century had the longest name?

Prince Sultan bin Salman bin Abdul Aziz Al-Saud, of Saudi Arabia (Shuttle mission 51-G, June 1985).

98. Where did the Russians get most of the dogs used for test subjects in rocket tests and space flights?

They picked up stray mongrels off the streets of Moscow.

99. At what airfield are the astronauts' aircraft based?

Ellington Field near Pasadena, Texas.

100. Who formed the first space camp outside the U. S.?

Patrick Baudry, a French astronaut (Shuttle mission 51-G) opened a space camp in France.

101. Where is the Russian mission control center?

At Kaliningrad, north of Moscow.

102. What is the name of the complex where the cosmonauts live and train?

Zvezdniy Gorodok (Star City) approximately 25 miles northeast of Moscow.

103. Why were gypsy moths taken into space on Skylab?

The U.S. Department of Agriculture had hopes to develop a sterile strain of moths to neutralize the destructive effects of the insect on Earth.

104. From what country are cosmonauts launched?

Kazakhstan, a republic of the former Soviet Union, but now an independent country.

105. What was the name of the Russian shuttle spacecraft?

Buran. In Russian, it means snowstorm or blizzard. It is now an exhibit in a playground park.

106. During what year was the first satellite, Sputnik 1, launched into Earth orbit?

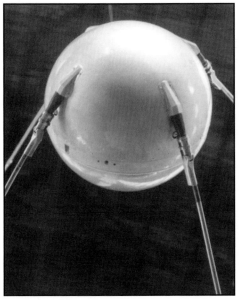

1957 (October 4). Sputnik is a combination of words meaning, "fellow-traveler of Earth."

Crazy Quote: *Commenting on Sputnik 1 and 2: "The satellite is little more than a scientific gimmick." Richard van der Riet Woolley, British Astronomer Royal, 1957*

107. What was Astronaut Virgil I. Grissom's nickname?

Gus.

108. What does NASA stand for?

National Aeronautics and Space Administration.

Sputnik 1 (mockup display at Paris Air Show).

109. Dr. C.C. (Chris) Kraft was in charge of the Mission Control Center during the Mercury, Gemini and most of the Apollo program. What do the initials C.C. stand for?

Christopher Columbus.

110. What year did NASA first start testing women to become astronauts?

1959. The project, sometimes referred to by the code name FLATS (First Lady Astronauts), was kept secret for three years and then dropped.

111. Who flew the first Shuttle into orbit?

John W. Young and Robert L. (Bob) Crippen, Columbia (STS-1), April 12, 1981.

Mysterious Polar Orbiter

Several hours after separating from Gemini 7, following the first rendezvous in space, Gemini 6A astronaut, Tom Stafford reported excitedly about a satellite going north to south and apparently ready to reenter. He got the attention of Frank Borman and Jim Lovell in the Gemini 7 spacecraft who began looking for this visitor. Then Wally played Jingle Bells using the harmonica while Tom Stafford jingled the bells in front of the microphone. It was December 15, 1965, ten days early for Santa, but the spirit of Christmas had come to space nevertheless.

112. What was the name of the very first communications satellite?

ECHO 1, launched August 12, 1960. It was a 100-foot metallic coated inflated sphere used to reflect (bounce) radio signals between ground stations. Transmissions were made between the U.S. and England. Because if its size, ECHO 1 was the first man-made satellite visible to ground observers.

113. What was the name of the first joint American/Russian manned space mission?

Apollo Soyuz Test Project, referred to as ASTP by the U.S. and SATP (Soyuz Apollo Test Project) by the Russians. It was flown in July 1975.

114. Which astronaut orbited the Moon during the first lunar landing by Armstrong and Aldrin?

Michael (Mike) Collins.

115. What was the name given to the first Lunar Module (LM) to land on the Moon?

Eagle, the LM flown by Neil Armstrong and Buzz Aldrin.

116. Who took the first musical instruments into space?

Wally Schirra (a tiny harmonica) and Tom Stafford (small bells), Gemini 6A, December 1967. *See sidebar,* **Mysterious Polar Orbiter.**

117. Which American astronaut amassed the most time in space during the 20th century?

Mission Specialist Shannon W. Lucid. (Just over 5,351 hours in Shuttles and the Mir space station.)

118. What item of Russian space food was shared by Cosmonaut Alexei Leonov with

Astronauts **Tom Stafford** and **Donald K. (Deke) Slayton** after the historic first docking between Russian and American spacecraft (Apollo-Soyuz, 1975)?

Borscht (a paste of beet soup contained in a tube).

119. The Shuttle Endeavour was named after the ship of what British explorer?

Captain James Cook who led an extensive exploration of the Pacific Ocean (18th century).

120. Who was the first person to orbit the Earth for more than a day?

Cosmonaut Gherman Titov (just over 24 hours on Vostok 2, August 6, 1961). He flew at age 25, still the youngest person to go into space (as of January 1, 2003).

121. Which astronaut holds the record for the most hours on space walks (EVAs) in the 20th century?

Jerry L. Ross (His cumulative time on space-walks was over 44 hours on seven EVAs). *See Q 510.*

122. Which Apollo mission had one of their three landing parachutes fail during descent?

Apollo 15. The splashdown was a bit rougher than normal, but no one was injured.

Photo of Wiley Post in suit.
(Courtesy of ConocoPhillips)

123. Who was the pilot who invented the first pressure suit (needed for high altitude flight)?

Wiley Post. In 1934 he flew to 50,000' and in the process encountered the jet stream.

InfoNote: Although Post wasn't the first to discover the jet stream, he was the first to make practical use of it to set speed records. In 1935 he flew from Burbank, California to Cleveland, Ohio averaging 280 miles per hour, almost 100 miles per hour faster than the maximum speed of his aircraft in still air.

124. Which astronaut changed his name (legally) after leaving the space program?

Edwin E. (Buzz) Aldrin legally changed his given name to Buzz.

125. What is the speed of the crawler-transporter as it carries the Shuttle to the launch pad?

One mile per hour. Even so, the driver must wear a seat belt. (Note: The speed up the 5-degree incline at the launch pad is ½ mile per hour and top speed when empty is 2 miles per hour.)

Photo of the crawler transporter (CT) with Shuttle.

126. How much does it cost to ferry the Shuttle from Edwards Air Force Base, California to the Shuttle Landing Facility at the Kennedy Space Center, Florida?

$ 750 thousand to $1 million dollars. I've seen both figures quoted.

Crazy Quote: *"I do not think it is at all probable that aeronautics will ever come into play as a serious modification of transport and communication." H.G. Wells (early science fiction author), 1902.*

Photo of Shuttle on NASA's Carrier Aircraft. *See Q 126.*

127. An airstrip on the Cape Canaveral Air Force station, used as an auxiliary landing field during the early space program, was originally called the Skid Strip. How did the name Skid Strip originate?

It was constructed at the Cape Canaveral Air Force Station in the early 1950s as a landing site for pilotless jet-powered Snark and Navaho winged cruise missiles some of which made remotely controlled landings by sliding (skidding) in on the runway (They had skids as landing gear.).

128. Who was the first African American Shuttle Commander?

Frederick D. (Fred) Gregory. He commanded STS-33 in November 1989.

129. Who was the first woman to fly as Pilot on the Shuttle?

Eileen M. Collins. Selected as a Pilot Astronaut in 1990, she flew as Shuttle Pilot on STS-63 (February 1995), STS-84 (May 1997) and as commander of STS-93 in July 1999.

130. Which crew was the first to transfer from one space station to another?

Cosmonauts Leonid Kizim and Vladimir Solovyev (from Mir to Salyut 7, 1986, using the Soyuz T-15 spacecraft).

First Base

Buzz called "Contact Light" based on a signal from the probe sensors that extended 5'-8" (1.7 meters) beneath front and side landing pads. The first probe sensor that touched the lunar surface turned on the contact light on the instrument panel. At this call, Neil was to shut down the descent engine. Because of the length of the probes it is unlikely the Lunar Module had touched down until after this call. Neil's full transmission was, "Houston, Tranquility base here. The Eagle has landed." spoken, just after touchdown.

The site of their landing was in the Sea of Tranquility, a large, relatively flat area near the center of the Moon's face, as we view it from Earth. Early astronomers who examined the Moon with telescopes noted large features that appeared relatively flat as compared to the surrounding surface features that looked like hilly or mountainous Earth features. They called the flat features, "mare" (pronounced mar'-eh), Latin for "sea".

131. How long does it take to orbit the Earth (under 300 miles altitude)?

Approximately 90 minutes (roughly 50 minutes in sunlight and 40 minutes in darkness).

132. What multi-purpose tool did all Skylab astronauts carry in their pockets?

A Swiss Army Knife.

133. What was the first word transmitted back to Earth from the Moon's surface? Who spoke it?

There is debate about this. "Contact" (spoken by Buzz Aldrin), or "Houston" (spoken by Neil Armstrong). *See sidebar,* **First Base**.

Crazy Quote: *Dr. Lee DeForest…predicted today that man will never reach the Moon, "regardless of all future scientific advances" … "To place a man in a multi-stage rocket and project him into the controlling gravitational field of the Moon,… perhaps land alive and then return to the Earth - all that constitutes a wild dream worthy of Jules Verne." Dr. Lee De Forest, "father of radio", San Francisco Chronicle 25 February 1957.*

134. The cremated remains of what geologist were taken to the Moon on the Lunar Prospector spacecraft?

Dr. Eugene Shoemaker, instrumental in geology training of Apollo astronauts. *See Q 31.*

135. Who were the first U.S. astronauts to be taught Russian by NASA-selected instructors?

Tom Stafford and Deke Slayton. Instruction started early 1973 to prepare them for the 1975 U.S./Soviet Apollo-Soyuz mission.

136. Which spacecraft was the first to have freezers to preserve food?

Skylab, America's first space station (1973-74).

137. Who was the first woman to fly in space?

Valentina Tereshkova, on Vostok 6, June 16, 1963. Her Call Sign was Chaika (Seagull).

138. Who was the first U.S. medical doctor to fly in space?

Dr. Joseph P. (Joe) Kerwin, Science Pilot for the Skylab 2 mission (first manned visit). Dr. Kerwin was a naval pilot and flight surgeon.

139. Who got the first haircut in space?

Paul J. (P.J.) Weitz. Pete Conrad was the first barber (Skylab 2, first manned mission to Skylab).

140. What Apollo-era crews were given medical and dental training in preparing for their flights?

The Skylab crews. Because of the long flights, planners anticipated the possibility of incurring injury, illness or dental problems.

141. All cosmonauts aboard the first generation Russian spacecraft, Vostok, made landings unlike all succeeding astronauts and cosmonauts. What was unique about their return to Earth?

They all ejected from the entry spacecraft and parachuted to the Earth's surface. *See Q 237.*

142. Which newspaper editorialized against the funding of rocket research by Dr. Robert Goddard?

The New York Times. In effect, the editorial promoted the erroneous notion that rocket engines can't work in a vacuum because the rocket exhaust doesn't have air to push against. The New York Times officially apologized to Goddard in 1969 (over 20 years after his death).

Crazy Quote : *"… Professor Goddard … does not know the relation of action to reaction, and of the need to have something better than a vacuum against which to react …he only seems to lack the knowledge ladled out daily in high schools…"* New York Times, January 18, 1920.

143. What special memorial did the Apollo 15 astronauts leave on the Moon?

It was called the Fallen Astronaut/Cosmonaut, a tiny sculpture of an astronaut in a space suit and a Commemorative Plaque inscribed with the names of all deceased astronauts/cosmonauts (as of July 1971). The names were listed in alphabetical order: Charles A. Bassett II, Pavel I. Belyayev, Roger B. Chaffee, Georgi Dobrovolsky, Theodore C. Freeman, Yuri A. Gagarin, Edward G. Givens, Jr., Virgil I. Grissom, Vladimir Komarov, Viktor Patsayev, Elliot M. See Jr., Vladislav Volkov, Edward H. White II, and Clifton C. Williams, Jr.

Photo of Commemorative Plaque and sculpture left on the Moon.

144. What was the first wheeled vehicle used on the Moon by astronauts?

The MET (Modular Equipment Transporter), a two-wheeled device similar to a golf cart. Apollo 14 astronauts Al Shepard and Ed Mitchell used it to deploy the lunar science experiments. *See sidebar,* **Flip-Flop**.

145. Which astronaut was the first to serve as NASA Administrator?

Shuttle Commander Richard H. (Dick) Truly.

146. What was the name of the nurse that supervised pre-flight physicals for Apollo astronauts?

Delores B. (Dee) O'Hara. Dee also was head nurse in Flight Medicine (clinic for astronauts and their families) at the Johnson Space Center and held this position through the Skylab missions. Her replacement was her good friend, Claudette Gage, who held the position for almost 25 years. *See Q 436.*

147. Which astronaut was instrumental in developing the F-117 stealth fighter?

Lt. General Tom Stafford. After leaving NASA, Tom returned to duty with the U.S. Air Force.

148. When did the first American spacecraft orbit another planet?

November 10, 1971, when Mariner 9 achieved orbit around Mars.

149. Yuri Gagarin, first human to orbit the Earth, died on March 27, 1968. What caused his death?

An air crash. His MIG-15 crashed during a routine training flight.

150. Which Apollo missions were canceled due to budgetary considerations?

Apollos 18, 19 & 20.

151. What was the first sporting event on the Moon?

A golf drive. *See sidebar*, **Fore!**

152 Who was the first African American to fly in space?

Guion S. (Guy) Bluford, Jr. (STS-8, 30 August 1983).

153. Which spacecraft sank in the Atlantic Ocean following splashdown?

Liberty Bell 7, after the second sub-orbital Mercury flight, flown by Gus Grissom July 21, 1961.

InfoNote: Liberty Bell 7 was recovered from the ocean floor and returned to the Kennedy Space Center on 21 July 1999, 38 years to the day after

Flip-Flop

I worked with a NASA engineer, Bill Creasy to develop the MET handle design. The original 2-handle design was sort of like pulling a wheelbarrow backwards (or a rickshaw). In 1/6 g, a person walking in a space suit (as on the Moon) tends to walk on tip-toes and waddle from side-to-side. When we used the 2-handle design version in 1/6 g simulations the "lunar waddle" caused us to rock the "golf cart" so violently that all the equipment and tools were shaken out of their restraints and thrown on the floor. We developed a yoke handle with a single triangular ring for the handgrip. It was coated with a high-friction material, called RTV, which enabled Ed and Al to pull the MET with a light grip and without shaking the contents onto the Moon. Incidentally, the MET was the only vehicle used on the Moon that was equipped with inflated rubber tires.

MET: (training model).

Fore!

After leaving NASA I was invited to speak to all sorts of groups and they all liked to ask questions. One question that I got frequently was about Al Shepard's golf shot. In 1983 I called Al when I was in Houston on business and he gave me some details I had never heard before. Al, Commander of Apollo 14, hit two golf balls using a standard 6-iron head (with a 2-inch stub) that was attached to a lunar soil sampling tool handle. This was done after all the surface exploration work was completed and he had gotten prior approval to try the shots. The cumbersome suit only permitted a one-armed swing. Ed Mitchell estimated the best drive went about 100 feet (phone conversation in the Spring of 2000). The second swing was a shank into the lunar surface.

Al said he got the idea while escorting entertainer Bob Hope on a tour of the Johnson Space Center. Bob carried a golf club, idly swinging the club while suspended in a rig that simulated lunar gravity (1/6 the Earth's). It was at this point that Al got the inspiration to try it in the real 1/6 g environment.

After the flight Al gave the "club" to the U.S. Golf Association Museum at Far Hill, New Jersey where it is now displayed. This rankled feelings at the Smithsonian Museum who wanted it for their space display. By rights they were supposed to get all "flown" space artifacts. After much wrangling the Smithsonian gave up. The "real McCoy" is in New Jersey and the display at the Smithsonian is a replica.

Incidentally, Ed Mitchell followed up Al's golf shots with his own "Lunar Olympics" effort. Not to be outdone, Ed grabbed a 6-foot pole that had been used to hold a solar wind experiment and threw it like a javelin at the spot where the golf ball had landed. He said it hit about a foot beyond the golf ball. Later Ed took a picture of the golf ball and "javelin" out the window of the Lunar Module. See photo in color section.

it sank. It is now on display at the Kansas Cosmophere and Space Center in Hutchinson, Kansas. See Q 734.

154. What did astronaut Ron Evans do at Star City to cause the arrival of Russian police?

He set off fireworks at dusk. It was July 4, 1974.

155. Which mission was referred to as the "handshake in space"?

The Apollo-Soyuz joint American-Soviet mission (July, 1975).

156. Which astronaut was imprisoned by the Japanese during World War II?

Mission Specialist Shannon Lucid. She and her missionary parents were interned in 1943.

157. Which American manned spacecraft was the first to splashdown in the Pacific ocean?

Mercury 8, Sigma 7, October 1962, flown by Wally Schirra.

158. What animals caused a launch delay of the Shuttle Discovery, STS-70 (June 1995)?

Woodpeckers. They pecked over a hundred holes (some up to four inches wide) in the external insulation covering the large External Tank (ET).

InfoNote: Because this delay was expensive in terms of time and money the Kennedy Space Center appealed to KSC employees and to the public for suggestions to prevent a recurrence of the woodpecker damage. The response was immediate and KSC had its answer, "owls." Artificial owls of all type (wood, plastic, inflated on tethers, statues, etc.) were placed on the Rotating Service Structure and the Fixed Service Structure in the vicinity of the ET. No subsequent problem with woodpeckers has occurred.

Woodpecker damage to the Shuttle's External Tank (left). The owl solution (right).

159. What unapproved food item was carried into space by the first Gemini crew?

A corned beef sandwich on rye with two slices of dill pickle. Wally Schirra bought it at "Wolfies", a deli in Cocoa Beach and put it in the refrigerator at the crew quarters. John Young picked it up and put it in his suit before launch.

160. Which astronauts flew the X-15 before joining NASA as astronauts?

Neil Armstrong and Joe Engle.

161. Who was the first person to ride a bicycle around the world?

Pete Conrad. He pedaled the Skylab stationary bicycle (ergometer) for just over 90 minutes, the time it takes to circle the globe.

162. In what year did the U.S. first launch a satellite?

1958. Explorer 1 on January 31. Dr. Wernher von Braun's team readied the Jupiter C booster in less than three months. The Jupiter C was a Redstone booster with a solid rocket assembly as an upper stage. See Q 798.

Neat Quote: "We can lick gravity but sometimes the paperwork is overwhelming." Dr. Wernher von Braun, circa 1957.

Wernher von Braun. *See Q 162.*

163. When were the first American women selected to become astronauts?

In January 1978, six women were among a group of 35, the eighth group of astronauts selected.

164. Who was the only astronaut who went to the Moon twice without landing on the Moon?

Jim Lovell on Apollo 8 and Apollo 13. Apollo 8 was only intended to orbit the Moon. Apollo 13 suffered an explosion and was forced to return without landing.

165. Who was the first African-American selected to become an astronaut?

U. S. Air Force Major Robert H. Lawrence was chosen in 1966 for the Manned Orbiting Laboratory program, a military project, later canceled. Major Lawrence was killed in a plane crash in December 1966.

166. What spacecraft had the first shower for bathing?

Skylab (1973-74). A half-gallon of hot water (per week) was provided for each shower.

167. What food did John Glenn eat during his Mercury flight?

Applesauce.

168. Which Shuttle crew complained of animal waste floating around in the spacecraft cabin?

The crew of Shuttle Mission 51B, (Spacelab 3, April 1985). The animal cages were provided with an exhaust airflow to evacuate and filter the air in the cages but it was too weak to do the job properly.

169. When was the first space rendezvous between manned spacecraft accomplished?

December 15, 1965. Gemini 6-A (Schirra and Stafford) executed the rendezvous with Gemini 7 (Borman and Lovell), and held position as close as six inches.

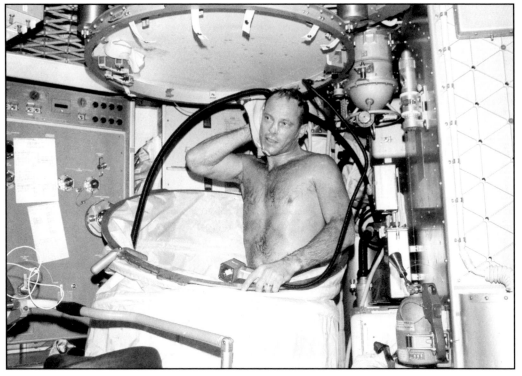

Jack R. Lousma taking a Skylab 3 shower. *See Q 166.*

170. What Apollo mission was struck by lightning shortly after liftoff?

Apollo 12, November 14, 1969. The strike temporarily upset the spacecraft navigational equipment but the Saturn V didn't even hiccup. The crew reached orbit without difficulty.

171. Which Shuttle made the first landing at the Kennedy Space Center in Florida?

Challenger, Commander Vance Brand (Shuttle mission 41-B, February 11, 1984).

172. What color did Al Shepard select for his custom Corvettes?

White.

173. Who was the first astronaut to launch on a Russian rocket?

Norman E. (Norm) Thagard, Soyuz TM-21, March 14, 1995, on a visit to the Russian Mir space station.

174. What spacecraft was selected as the first escape "lifeboat" for crews on the International Space Station?

The Russian Soyuz spacecraft.

175. Who was the first Canadian to fly in space?

Marc Garneau (Shuttle Mission 41G, October 1984).

176. When was the U.S. flag first applied to a space suit?

In June 1965. Gemini 4 astronauts McDivitt and White had flags added to their space suits.

177. The majority of Earth-orbiting satellites are used for what purpose?

Communications (television, telephone and data links).

Crazy Quote: *"… there is practically no chance communications space satellites will be used to provide better telephone, telegraph, television or radio service inside the United States."*
T. M. Craven, Federal Communications Commission, 1961.

178. What group of astronauts joined NASA without going through the NASA selection procedure?

The seventh group in August 1969.

InfoNote: When the military (Department of Defense) Manned Orbiting Laboratory (MOL) program was canceled seven of the MOL astronauts were transferred to NASA. They had already gone through a rigorous selection procedure earlier. Astronauts Bobko, Crippen, Fullerton, Hartsfield, Overmyer, Peterson and Truly participated in Shuttle program development and all flew on the Shuttle.

179. What manned spacecraft had the first flight computer (operated by the crew)?

Gemini.

180. Why did Skylab astronauts wear shoes with a triangular metal cleat attached to the sole?

The cleat attached to a grid structure and was used to hold the crewmen in place at work sites.

181. What design feature of the Shuttle hand-held cameras eliminates the problem of film fogging (caused by radiation)?

It's a digital camera so there is no film to be damaged by radiation. Images are recorded electronically, stored on a disk and can be transmitted to the ground during flight.

182. Which Apollo crew was the first to use the Lunar Roving Vehicle (LRV) , an electric powered "dune buggy," during their exploration of the Moon?

The Apollo 15 crew (Dave Scott and Jim Irwin).

Photo of Apollo 15 Lunar Roving Vehicle (LRV).

183. Which manned spacecraft was the first to be able to change its orbit (Exclude retrofire for de-orbit.)?

Gemini 3, March 1965.

184. Which astronaut became an artist after leaving NASA?

Alan L. (Al) Bean. He was the fourth Moon walker (Apollo 12) and commander of the Skylab 3 mission. Al has become a very successful artist specializing in artistic interpretation of the Apollo missions.

185. Who was the first woman to do a space-walk?

Cosmonaut Svetlana Savitskaya (July 1984).

186. What spacecraft provided the first television views of the Earth?

Explorer 6 (August 1959).

187. What city turned its lights on and off to signal an astronaut flying overhead?

Perth, Australia. Gordon Cooper viewed the lights. Mercury 9, Faith 7, May 1963.

188. Gemini astronauts participated in what sport tradition in the Houston Astrodome on April 12, 1965?

The ceremonial first pitch to kick off the Houston Astros' baseball season (their first game in the new stadium). On April 23, 1999, Neil Armstrong (who had participated in the 1965 event) threw out the first pitch for the opening game of the last year the Astros played in the Astrodome.

189. When did the last Apollo crew land on the Moon?

December 10, 1972 (Apollo 17).

190. How long did it take the Apollo astronauts to get from the Earth to the Moon?

About 3½ days.

191. On which Shuttle flight did an Arabian prince fly as a Payload Specialist?

STS-51-G (June 1985); Prince Sultan Al-Saud of Saudia Arabi.

192. Which astronauts landed near another U.S. spacecraft, already on the Moon?

Pete Conrad and Al Bean (Apollo 12, November 1969). *See sidebar,* **Bull's-eye!**

193. Who was the first person to transmit television from a spacecraft to Earth?

Cosmonaut Andrian Nikolayev from Vostok 3 in August 1962.

194. Which Apollo astronaut was removed from the crew shortly before launch because of exposure to a contagious disease?

Thomas K. (Ken or T.K.) Mattingly. He was replaced by John L. (Jack) Swigert on the Apollo 13 crew because of Ken's exposure to rubella (3-day measles).

195. Who was the first person to fly into space twice?

Gus Grissom (Mercury 4 and Gemini 3). Wally Schirra was the first to make 2 orbital flights.

196. What does the acronym, "SETI," stand for?

Search for Extraterrestrial Intelligence.

197. Who was the first person to experience space sickness?

Cosmonaut Gherman Titov (Vostok 2, August 1961).

198. What was the mission number (designation) of the first Shuttle flight following the loss of the Challenger?

STS-26, Shuttle Discovery, September 1988, 20 months after the loss of the Challenger (51-L).

199. Who was the first cosmonaut to fly aboard the U.S. Shuttle?

Sergei Krikalev, February 1994, STS-60 aboard Shuttle Discovery.

200. Who was the first woman to pilot an aircraft faster than the speed of sound?

Jacqueline Cochran, flying a Canadian F-86 (1950).

201. Which Apollo crew was the first to transmit color television from the Moon?

Apollo 12. Astronauts Alan Bean and Pete Conrad, November 1969.

202. Who was called the Führer of the launch pad?

Guenter Wendt, who exerted strict control of the

Bull's-eye!

One of Apollo 12's objectives was to test navigation accuracy by aiming their landing for a specific relic (Surveyor 3) whose position on the lunar surface was known. Pete and Al landed within 600 feet of the spacecraft, which had soft-landed on the Moon 2½ years earlier in 1967. They removed the Surveyor's TV camera and lunar soil scoop and returned them to be analyzed to determine the effects of exposure to the harsh lunar environment.

Conrad examining the Surveyor spacecraft TV camera.

White Room positioned adjacent to the spacecraft hatch on the launch pad. *See Q 37 and Q 83.*

203. Who were the first astronauts to do a space-walk from the Shuttle?

Story Musgrave and Donald H. (Don) Peterson (STS-6, April 1983).

204. The first three Russian manned spacecraft were named Vostok, Voskhod & Soyuz. What do these names mean in English?

Vostok = east; Voskhod = sunrise; Soyuz = union.

205. Who was the last person to fly solo around the Moon in the 20th century?

Ron Evans, Apollo 17, December 1972.

206. First space-walker Alexi Leonev barely managed to reenter his airlock because his suit was too stiff. How did he overcome this problem?

He operated a valve on the suit and dropped the internal pressure of the suit to decrease suit stiffness.

207. How does the Shuttle generate electrical power?

By fuel cells. They combine oxygen and hydrogen to produce electricity and drinking water.

208. What was the largest tool in the Apollo survival kit?

A fifteen-inch stainless steel machete.

209. Who made the first flight away from and independent of the mother ship during a spacewalk in Earth orbit?

Astronaut Bruce McCandless II, Shuttle mission 41-B (February 1984), during the first test of the Manned Maneuvering Unit (MMU).

210. What spacecraft was the first to orbit the Moon and return to Earth?

Zond 5 (September 1968). Unmanned Zond missions were pathfinders for planned Soviet manned lunar flights.

211. Which Shuttle was the first to land at a site that wasn't in California or Florida?

McCandless flying the Manned Maneuvering Unit (MMU). *See Q 209.*

Columbia. On STS-3, the 3rd Shuttle flight, Columbia was diverted from Edwards AFB because of heavy rains there. Commander Jack Lousma and Pilot Gordon (or Gordo) Fullerton landed on a backup strip at the White Sands Space Harbor near Alamogordo, New Mexico. *See Q 366.*

212.   Which was the first backup crew to replace a prime crew for a space mission?

The Gemini 9 backup crew (Tom Stafford and Gene Cernan, June 1966). The prime crew (Elliot M. See, Jr. and Charles Bassett II) were killed in a plane crash four months before flight.

213.   What is the official term for the Shuttle robot arm operated by the astronauts?

The RMS (Remote Manipulator System) or SRMS (Shuttle RMS). The designation SRMS was introduced to distinguish it from the SSRMS (International Space Station RMS, used on the ISS). *See Q 560.*

214. What was the internal habitable volume of Skylab, America's first space station?

Photo of Remote Manipulator System on the International Space Station (upper right). *See Q 213.*

Approximately 12,500 cubic feet, roughly the same volume of a house with 1,500 square feet of floor space (Count it correct if you're within 1,000 cubic feet). *See Q 336.*

215. What was the name of the Soviet remotely controlled vehicle used to explore the Moon's surface?

Lunokhod. (Lunokhod 1 landed in November 1970. Lunokhod 2 followed in January 1973)

216. How many wheels did the Lunokhod have?

Eight.

217. What was the record for the longest manned space flight of the 20th century?

438 days. On 22 March 1995, cosmonaut Valery V. Polyokov returned after spending a record 14½ months aboard the Mir space station. That's approximately 7,000 orbits.

Crazy Quote: "…*three orbits may very well be the threshold of tolerable endurance for weightlessness for man in space." Lillian Levy, science reporter, Washington Daily News, June 12, 1962.*

218. Where did Mercury, Gemini and Apollo era astronauts go for tropical survival training?

The jungle of Panama.

219. When was the first 3-man space-walk conducted in the U.S. space Program?

On 13 May 1992 three astronauts (Rick Hieb, Pierre Thuot and Tom Akers) were needed to manhandle the Intelsat 6 satellite to stabilize it for repair work in the Shuttle payload bay. This was on Shuttle mission STS-49, the first launch of the Shuttle, Endeavour. *See Q 347.*

220. Who was the first child born on Earth whose parents had both flown in space?

Yelena, daughter of cosmonauts Andrian G. Nikolayev and Valentina V. Tereshkova.

221. In what spacecraft did the crewmembers stand up to fly it?

The Apollo Lunar Module (LM). *See sidebar,* **Stand-up Guys**.

222. How many Shuttle launch pads are there at the Kennedy Space Center?

Two. Pads 39A and 39B, were originally prepared in the mid 1960s for the Apollo Saturn rockets.

223. What did Skylab crewmembers do with their dirty clothes?

Dirty clothes were discarded with trash. *See Q 226.*

224. Who was the first American woman to fly in space?

Sally Ride, on Shuttle Mission STS-7, in June, 1983.

Stand-up Guys

The LM (pronounced "Lem") had no seats or couches (to save weight and space). During descent to the Moon's surface and ascent back to lunar orbit, the astronauts were held down toward the floor by straps (tethers) attached to both sides of their suits near the waist. During the weightless phases the tethers kept them from floating away from the floor of the LM.

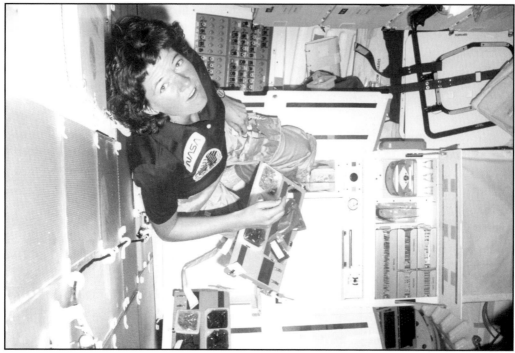

Photo of Sally Ride. *See Q 224.*

225. When did the first fatality occur in the U.S. astronaut corps?

On October 31, 1964 Theodore C. (Ted) Freeman was killed when a snow goose slammed through the windshield of his T-38 jet trainer (near Ellington Air Force Base, Houston, Texas).

226. Where did Skylab astronauts dispose of their trash?

In a large empty Oxygen tank at the rear of the main section of Skylab (Tank volume was 2,500 cubic feet [70 cubic meters], about the size of a one-car garage.). Because the "dumpster" tank was at a vacuum, an airlock (Trash Airlock or TAL) was required to transfer the trash from the aft crew compartment into the tank. *See Q 223.*

227. Who performed the first glide test of the Shuttle Enterprise?

Astronauts Fred Haise and Gordon Fullerton, Aug 12, 1977. The Enterprise was released from the back of a Boeing 747 at 23,000 feet and glided six miles to land at Edwards Air Force Base, California. *See Q 12 and Q 333.*

228. What manufacturer built the Space Shuttle?

Rockwell International (now Boeing North American), with the help of thousands of subcontractors and suppliers across the U.S.

229. What spacecraft was the first to carry four crewmen?

Shuttle Enterprise being released from the carrier aircraft for Approach and Landing tests. *See Q 227.*

Shuttle Columbia (STS-5, November 1, 1982). It was manned by astronauts Vance Brand, Bob Overmyer, Joe Allen and Bill Lenoir.

230. How many tiles are attached to the Shuttle to protect it from reentry heating?

Approximately 31,000 (each attached by hand).

231. What name had NASA originally selected for the Shuttle, Enterprise?

Constitution. The name was changed on direction from the White House after a vigorous letter writing campaign by devoted fans of Star Trek who wanted it named after the fictional starship of the TV series.

232. How many pounds of lunar rocks were brought back by the six crews who landed on the Moon?

837 pounds. This included 2,196 rock samples and stray particles of lunar dust.

233. Who was the last person to stand on the Moon in the 20th century?

Gene Cernan. Gene was commander of Apollo 17, December 1972.

234. Russian space stations have been named Salyut and Mir. What do these names mean in English?

Salyut = salute (a salute to the 10th anniversary of Yuri Gagarin's flight). Mir = peace.

235. How much did the Apollo program cost?

Cost is officially estimated at $23.5 billion (That would be 95 billion dollars in the year 2000).

236. What NASA award for exceptional performance must be presented personally by an astronaut?

The Silver Snoopy. It's a lapel pin of sterling silver, depicting the Peanuts© comic strip character, Snoopy, (a beagle) in a space suit.

237. Who was the first human space traveler to land on the Earth's surface while still in his spacecraft?

Alan B. (Al) Shepard, Mercury 3. *See Q 141.*

238. What was common to the names given to the manned Mercury spacecraft?

The numeral 7. *See Appendix A:* **Naming Spacecraft.**

239. Can a spider spin a web in zero-gravity?

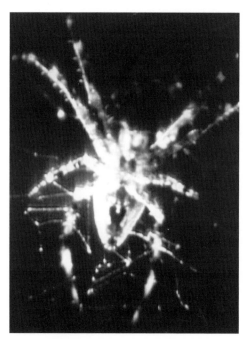

Photo of "Arabella" the spider.

Yes. Both spiders taken into space by the second Skylab crew, were able to spin webs. *See Q 294*

240. Who was the first woman to make five space flights?

Mission Specialist Shannon Lucid. *See Q 628.*

241. In what direction does an astronaut look to see meteors?

Down toward the Earth. The meteor streak occurs as the meteoroid enters the atmosphere at an altitude of approximately 50 miles, which is well below spacecraft altitude.

242. Who were the first married couple in the U.S. astronaut corps?

Anna L. and William F. (Bill) Fisher. Anna was selected in 1978 and Bill in 1980.

243. What was the name given to the first manned Gemini spacecraft?

Molly Brown. *See sidebar,* **What's in a Name?**

244. How long was the suit hose (Life Support Umbilical) for Skylab EVAs (space-walks)?

60 feet. It supplied oxygen, chilled water (circulated through tubing in a garment to cool the crewmen), communications and data conductors plus a steel cable to add strength to the hose.

245. Who was the first astronaut to capture a satellite by using the Manned Maneuvering Unit (MMU)?

Joseph P. (Joe) Allen. Joe captured the Palapa satellite (Shuttle mission 51-A, November 1984).

246. What is the length of the Shuttle's External Tank (ET)?

154 feet. Its diameter is 28.6 feet.

247. When was NASA formed?

October 1, 1958. NASA was derived from the NACA (National Advisory Committee for Aeronautics).

248. How many astronauts were chosen in the first selection?

Seven (often referred to as The Original Seven) *See Q 270.*

249. What was the name of America's first manned space program?

Mercury or Project Mercury.

What's In a Name?

Virgil I. (Gus) Grissom flew the second Mercury sub-orbital flight in a spacecraft he named Liberty Bell 7. After landing in the Atlantic the hatch inexplicably blew off and the spacecraft began taking on water. Gus climbed out, got into the water and started having a problem of his own. His suit began filling with water and the chopper pilot diverted from trying to recover the spacecraft to work on saving Gus. In so doing the spacecraft sank. Gus was chagrined at the entire turn of events. *See Q 734 and Q 153.*

Later Gus was assigned as commander of the first Gemini mission (Gemini 3) and coined a suitable name for the spacecraft he and John Young would fly. The name Molly Brown was his choice (from the stage show, "The Unsinkable Molly Brown"). It seemed entirely appropriate and innocent enough but someone at NASA headquarters thought the name was a bit frivolous so they ordered him to submit another name.

He said, "OK, I'll call it the Titanic". Gus got his way - Molly Brown was approved. After that, none of the other Gemini crews were permitted to name their spacecraft and simply used their mission designations (Gemini 4 through Gemini 12). Starting with Apollo 9, astronauts were once again permitted to name their spacecraft but the practice ended with Apollo 17. *See Appendix A:* **Naming Spacecraft.**.

250. What indelicate name have the astronauts given to the KC-135 jet aircraft they use to experience zero gravity?

The Vomit Comet. It's also been called the K-bird and Barf Buzzard.

InfoNote: The KC-135 aircraft flies a roller coaster path (zooms, pushovers and dives) to create brief periods (25-30 seconds) of zero gravity. The purpose of these flights is to familiarize astronauts with weightlessness and to evaluate equipment and procedures. All these ups and downs cause some people to become nauseated, hence the unflattering name.

A Virginia company sells "tourist" rides for zero-g flights in Russia on an Ilyushin aircraft at a cost of $5,400 per head. A French company offers commercial zero-g services in an Airbus 300 and a U. S. company received approval in 2002 to operate a Boeing 727 for zero-g flights catering to movie companies and also to the public.

Photo of the K-bird (The Vomit Comet) diving.

251. What bizarre devices were proposed to bring the Mercury spacecraft out of orbit if the retro-braking rockets failed to fire?

Two approaches were proposed: a) an inflatable balloon and, b) a kite tail similar to a

Chinese dragon kite tail. Both of these were trailing drag devices whose purpose was to bring the Mercury spacecraft down in less than 24 hours.

252. What is the name of the Texas road (off I-45), that leads to the Johnson Space Center?

NASA Road 1.

253. Which astronaut later became an aquanaut by exploring the ocean floor?

Scott Carpenter. He spent 30 days on the ocean floor in Sealab II.

254. Which spacecraft was the first to send back television pictures of the lunar surface?

The Soviet Luna 9 (February 3, 1966).

255. In November 1973 astronauts and cosmonauts engaged in what kind of a fight?

A friendly snowball fight (during a rest stop while traveling from Star City to Moscow).

256. What is the name given to the process of transmitting technical data to or from spacecraft?

Telemetry.

Skylab 3 wives' patch.
(artwork & photo courtesy of Ardis Shanks)

257. The wives of what crew were honored by receiving their own mission patch?

Skylab 3 (2nd visit: Bean, Lousma and Garriott).

InfoNote: The official patch featured a rendition of Leonardo DaVinci's human form drawing, also called the Vitruvian man (a male figure proportional graphic related to the circle and square, suggested by the Roman architect, Vitruvius). The wives' patch, created by artist, Ardis Shanks, was a spoof featuring a woman in place of the man. The names of the wives circle the top of the patch: Sue (Bean), Helen-Mary (Garriott) and Gratia (Lousma).

Left to right: Helen-Mary Garriott, Sue Bean, Ardis Shanks (artist) and Gratia Lousma. *See Q 257*

258. Why were NASA's Apollo Saturn booster assembly and test sites (in Alabama and Mississippi) located along rivers that had access to the sea?

All except the S-IVB Saturn stages were too large to be shipped by land. They were hauled to and from the Marshall Space Flight Center (MSFC) on barges along the Tennessee and Mississippi rivers, across the Gulf of Mexico, around the tip of Florida and up the Atlantic Ocean to Cape Canaveral, making maximum use of the Intracoastal Waterway. The S-IVB stage could be shipped by barge or aircraft. *See Q 573*.

259. What was the name of the aircraft used to ship the third stage (S-IVB) of a Saturn V rocket?

The Super Guppy. It was a Boeing C-97 with the fuselage enlarged to hold the 21' diameter S-IVB. The Super Guppy was also used to ship Apollo spacecraft (the Command-Service Module, and the Lunar Module) from manufacturing plants in Long Island (LM) and California (CSM).

Crazy Quote: *"By no possibility can carriage of freight or passengers through mid-air compete with their carriage on the Earth's surface."* unsigned editorial, Engineering News 1908.

260. Which Apollo Earth-orbiting manned mission was launched by a Saturn V?

Apollo 9. The crew performed all the tasks involving the Lunar Module (LM) that would be required for a successful Moon landing and retrieval of the LM in lunar orbit.

Photo of NASA's Super Guppy transport aircraft.

261. Who was the first astronaut to exercise in space?

Wally Schirra, Mercury 8, Sigma 7, October 1962. He exercised using an elastic bungee cord.

262. Why did the first Manned Maneuvering Unit (MMU) have to be replaced by the backup unit?

While the MMU was being transported from Denver to Florida by truck, the driver ran off the road and overturned. The extent of damage to the MMU was uncertain and the backup unit was readied for flight to avoid a possible problem.

263. What is the name of the flight controller who gave the OK to continue the first Moon landing when computer alarms in the Lunar Module were confusing and distracting the crew?

Steven Bales, the flight controller responsible for monitoring LM computer performance.

264. Who tested the prototype of the Manned Maneuvering Unit (MMU) in space?

The last two Skylab crews.

InfoNote: It was called the Astronaut Maneuvering Unit (AMU) and was flown inside the Skylab to evaluate controls and handling properties. The engines on the AMU used nitrogen gas. The AMU was also known by two other names: ASMU (Automatically Stabilized Maneuvering Unit) and M-509 (the experiment number associated with evaluations of the AMU). This was the first time a spacecraft was flown inside another spacecraft.

265. What suit feature enables observers to identify crewmembers during two-person space-walks?

The suit of one crewmember has red stripes around the legs (mid-thigh).

266. What device was used to create high "g" forces during the training of the early astronauts?

A centrifuge. A pivoting enclosure on the end of a rotating arm could generate forces on the body up to 16 times normal gravity (a 16 g force, eyeballs in). *See Appendix C:* **g-Forces**

267. Which Apollo mission patch (insignia) did not have the astronaut's names on the design?

The insignia for Apollo 11, the first Moon landing mission. Names were excluded as a gesture of respect for all the unrecognized contributors to the mission.

268. What was the original name given to the Gemini program?

Mercury Mark II.

269. Which was the first space project to require body tattoos on the astronauts?

Mercury.

InfoNote: The tattoos were black ink dots used to identify the locations (chest and back) for placement of biomedical sensors (for medical and physiological monitoring). On Skylab, it was my job to attach biosensors to Ed Gibson for his tests and I really had a problem. Ed had dark freckles on his back and it was hard to tell which mark was the NASA tattoo.

270. In what year was the first group of astronauts selected?

Names of the first seven were announced in May 1959. *See Q 248.*

271. What is space sight, a term coined by cosmonauts?

A validated improvement in vision while viewing the Earth from orbit. See *sidebar*, **The Eyes Have It**.

272. When President Eisenhower approved the creation of a manned space program what one professional qualification did he specify that astronauts should have?

He insisted that they should be selected from active duty military test pilots.

273. Which Shuttle commander flew in space before joining NASA?

Joe H. Engle. Joe qualified as an astronaut when he flew the X-15 rocket plane above 50 miles altitude, the U.S. definition of the space boundary. Other countries use 100 kilometers (62 miles) as the boundary.

274. What was the name of the first Japanese satellite?

Ohsumi, launched February 11, 1970.

275. Who accomplished the first crew-controlled docking in space?

Neil Armstrong and Dave Scott (Gemini 8, March 1966) with an Agena target vehicle. *See Q 18.*

276. Which Shuttle Commander made the first night launch?

Dick Truly (STS-8, August 30, 1983). He also made the first night landing at the end of this mission.

277. Why were two astronauts "bumped" from their assignments to visit the Russian Mir space station?

One was too tall and one was too short to fit properly (for safety) in the couches of the Russian Soyuz spacecraft used as a shuttle to and from the Mir space station. One Soyuz was always docked

The Eyes Have It

After about 3-4 months in orbit the cosmonauts reported better vision (resolution and color discrimination) and proved it in tests devised by scientists on the ground. In actual tests cosmonauts have identified features as small as 30 meters across (approximately 100 feet across) from about 200-250 miles altitude. This is the space equivalent of a hunter developing a trained eye.

The Tall & Short Of It

During selection of the fifth group (1966) Marine Jack Lousma got very creative when filling out his application form for astronaut selection. He listed his height as five feet-thirteen inches (and made the cut!). The astronaut height limits of 5' 11" for Mercury and 6' for Gemini and Apollo was dictated by the size of the spacecraft and the crew couches. But it could be fudged a bit. For Shuttle astronauts the height limits are more flexible. The limits are 64"-76" for Pilots; and 60" - 76" for Mission Specialists.

However, a more restrictive height limitation applied for the first few years of operation onboard the International Space Station (ISS) while the lifeboat was a standard model of the Russian-built Soyuz. See Q 277. Prior to the introduction of the Soyuz TMA (late 2002), the height limitations were: minimum: 164 cm (64½ "), maximum: 186 cm (73¼"). These limitations disqualified over half the U. S. astronauts from long-term stays aboard the ISS. For example, they could go up on Shuttle visits to the ISS but also had to come back when it returned.

In 1996 NASA contracted with the Russians ($39 million) to make these changes. NASA's contribution paid for the design changes and the Russians swallowed the construction cost. With the introduction of the Soyuz TMA the new height restrictions accommodated 90% of the U. S. astronaut population. The height limits (starting in late 2002) were changed to minimum 59" (150 cm) to a maximum of 74.8" (190 cm).

to the Mir for routine crew rotation but it also serves as a standby spacecraft for emergency evacuation from the Mir. See Q 279.

278. What was the height limit for the selection of the Mercury astronauts?

Five feet eleven inches.

279. What was the maximum height limitation for astronauts selected for Apollo?

Six feet. (Some outstanding candidates were just over the limit and were selected anyway). See sidebar, **The Tall & Short Of It**, for height limits established for the various U.S. space programs.

280. Who was the first person from India to go into space?

Cosmonaut Rakesh Sharma (Soyuz T-11, 1984).

281. Where is the "Astronaut Viewing Area"?

At the Kennedy Space Center, Florida. It's a private site where astronauts, their families and guests can view launches.

282. What building at the Kennedy Space Center do astronauts call the beach house?

It's a house remotely located on the beach where astronauts hold private briefings and conferences. It's also used to meet with families and friends to relax during preparations before launch.

283. What happened to the chimpanzees, Ham and Enos, who flew in Mercury spacecraft tests in the early 1960s?

They died of natural causes; Ham in 1983 at the North Carolina Zoo and Enos in 1962 at Holloman Air Force Base, New Mexico.

284. What part of the U.S. did the Soviet space planners (1970s -1990s) designate as an emergency landing site for cosmonauts?

Left to right: chimpanzees "Ham" & "Enos". See Q 283.

The U.S. Midwest and north-central plains (North Dakota to Kansas/Nebraska to Illinois). It is relatively flat terrain and is available for those orbits that don't permit landing on their primary site in Kazakhstan. NASA was unaware of this contingency plan for many years. Other emergency sites include Western Europe and the Sea of Okhotsk off the east coast of Russia.
See Q 328 sidebar.

285. What near-disaster occurred during the unmanned launch of the Skylab space station?

A meteoroid debris shield tore away ripping off one of the solar wings from the side of the space station and a part of the shield wrapped around the other wing preventing its automatic deployment. *See Q 385.*

286. Who was the first person to orbit the Earth?

Cosmonaut Yuri Gagarin, aboard Vostok, April 12, 1961.

Crazy Quote: *"Space Travel is utter bilge." Richard van der Riet Woolley, British Astronomer Royal, 1956. His predecessor, was more optimistic, predicting man would travel into space, "about 200 to 300 years from now." Harold Jones, 1956.*

287. Which Soviet manned space mission was the first to land on a body of water?

Soyuz 23. Unable to dock with the Salyut 5 space station, Cosmonauts Zudov and

Rozhdestvensky had to execute an emergency reentry and landed on a frozen lake (Lake Tengiz) in the middle of a blizzard (October 16, 1976). *See Q 62.*

288. What official commemorative item was left on the Moon by the first crew to land there?

A plaque. It was inscribed with the words, *Here Men From The Planet Earth First Set Foot Upon the Moon. July 1969 AD. We Came in Peace For All Mankind.* The plaque was attached beneath the ladder on the front leg or landing strut of the Lunar Module. *See Q 374.*

Photo of Apollo 11 Commemorative Plaque.

289. In addition to the crew, whose name appears on the Apollo 11 commemorative plaque?

President Richard Nixon. The middle initial, M, was removed when the White House reviewed the design.

290. What Shuttle crewmember carried a flute to space (and played it for recreation)?

Mission Specialist Ellen Ochoa (STS-56, April 1993). *See Q 738.*

291. Why did Astronaut Deke Slayton, in charge of the Flight Crew Directorate, have the trampoline removed from the Astronaut Gym (1967)?

Ellen Ochoa. See Q 290

Walt Cunningham, while in training as a prime crewman for Apollo 7, broke a vertebra in his neck during a spirited workout on the trampoline. Walt wore a neck brace for several weeks but recovered quickly, continued training and made the Apollo 7 flight.

292. What NASA media representative, dubbed The Voice of Mercury, introduced the term, "A-OK"?

U. S. Air Force Lt. Col. John A. (Shorty) Powers. The term "A-OK" was not used by astronauts, NASA Flight Controllers or Directors. Shorty had picked up the term from communications technicians in Florida.

293. Who is the only person allowed to communicate directly with astronauts to discuss operational issues?

The astronaut serving as CapCom (Capsule Communicator) in the Mission Control Center (MCC).

294. What were the names given to the first spiders in space (Name one.)?

Arabella and Anita (second Skylab mission). *See Q 239.*

295. Who was the first astronaut from Mexico?

Rodolfo Neri-Vela (STS 61B, November 1985).

296. Prior to Apollo, which space crew held the altitude record for space flight?

Gemini 11 Astronauts Conrad and Gordon (850 miles above the Earth).

297. What caused a disagreement between cosmonauts and Soviet space physiologists prior to Gagarin's flight?

The doctors sought to disable the manual controls of the Vostok spacecraft. *See sidebar,* **The Lockout**.

298. Which U.S. space program was the first to invite U.S. high school students to propose experiments to be performed in space?

The Lockout

Although Soviet space physicians had recovered dogs from space missions, and the data indicated satisfactory adaptation to the weightless condition, the doctors were very apprehensive about Gagarin's ability to perform duties in space. Some thought that psychological stress during the flight would cause him to become irrational in behavior and be incapable of controlling the spacecraft or, worse still, he would interfere with the autopilot, which was the primary mode of controlling the flight. At first, the doctors ordered deactivation of manual controls so that Gagarin would be unable to do anything even if he were so disposed. Essentially reduced to the role of a lab rat, the cosmonaut objected and pointed to two earlier failures of the autopilot. A bizarre compromise was reached.

A "logic clock," which we would call a combinaion lock, was installed in the Vostok spacecraft to prevent the cosmonaut from enabling manual control. The doctors promised to transmit the combination to Gagarin if the autopilot failed. At this point Sergeyev Korolev, chief designer of the Soviet space program, intervened for the cosmonauts. He pointed out that a radio failure was more likely than a failure of the automatic pilot.

Gagarin memorized half of the combination and Korolev directed that the other half of the combination be placed in an envelope and fastened to the wall of the spacecraft, available for use if the autopilot failed. The autopilot functioned normally and Gagarin never had to use the combination for the lock. This incident did little to foster good will between the cosmonauts and the Soviet doctors. As a matter of trivia the three "missing" digits (placed in the envelope) were, 1-2-5. The three digits memorized by Gagarin were 1-4-5.

Skylab (1973-74). The Skylab Student Project included nineteen approved experiments.

299. Who was Spain's first astronaut?

Pedro Duque (STS-95, November 1998).

300. Who was CapCom (Spacecraft Communicator) when the first lunar landing was made?

Charles M. (Charlie) Duke, Jr. Charlie later landed on the Moon on Apollo 16.

301. Whom did the media refer to as the astronauts' personal physician?

Dr. Charles E. (Chuck) Berry.

302. Who performed the first space-walk in "deep space"?

Al Worden, Apollo 15, August 1971, on the Apollo 15 return trip from the Moon.

303. What is the designation (name) of the suits worn by Shuttle astronauts during launch (and reentry)?

Launch and Entry Suits (LES) The LES was introduced after the loss of the Challenger.

304. Which Apollo era astronaut had the most sets of twin children?

Jerry Carr (two sets of twins).

305. Which U.S. space crew was the first to carry coffee as a beverage?

Apollo 7. They had a hot water dispenser used to inject water into plastic drink bags containing instant coffee.

306. What crew was the first to celebrate Thanksgiving, Christmas and New Years in space?

The Skylab 4 crew, November 1973 - February 1974. (Carr, Gibson and Pogue). *See sidebar,* **Holiday Spirit**.

307. What is the name of the experiment that enables American students to talk directly to Shuttle astronauts?

SAREX (Shuttle Amateur Radio Experiment).

308. Who was the first Native American to fly in space?

John B. Harrington, a member of the Chickasaw tribe, flew as Pilot on Shuttle mission STS-113, November, 2002.

309. How many orbits did the Skylab space station make before reentering the atmosphere?

34,981. Skylab was launched May 14, 1973 and reentry occurred July 11, 1979.

310. In what country did pieces of Skylab land?

Australia. Fortunately, most of the debris landed in the Indian Ocean but some pieces survived reentry and hit in western Australia near Perth. *See sidebar,* **Chicken Little Down Under**.

311. What kind of seeds did Stuart A. (Stu) Roosa carry on the Apollo 14 mission?

Several types of tree seeds.

InfoNote: After the flight the tree seeds were incubated at the Johnson Space Center to create seedlings to be planted as commemorative trees. During a summer weekend the air conditioning failed and most of the seedlings died. The hardy American Sycamore seedlings survived along with a few others. Most of the Apollo 14 commemorative trees planted at various NASA facilities are Sycamores.

Holiday Spirit

Only two U.S. crews celebrated Christmas in space during the 20th century, Apollo 8 (Borman, Lovell and Anders - December 1968), and our flight. For us, there were tiny presents hidden on board (from our wives) and a rollout Christmas tree made of fabric, which we attached to food lockers. We had already made a tree from food cans (See Q 67). My present was a tie tack. Jerry and I had completed a strenuous 7-hour space walk on Christmas day and we really enjoyed relaxing at the end of that long spacewalk.

Chicken Little Down Under

During a Q & A session at the Kennedy Space Center Visitor Complex in 2002, I was asked, "Where did Skylab land?" I answered that most all landed in the Indian Ocean with a few pieces hitting in an unpopulated region of Western Australia. A man gestured for the microphone from the person who was handling the audience participation. He said, "One piece landed on my brother's roof and another in my back yard." "My brother got a free trip to America to claim a prize that had been offered for the first person to turn in a (validated) piece of Skylab debris. He was supposed to get a $5,000 prize in addition, but never received it. Yet he felt the trip to America was fitting compensation." Now when someone asks the question I recite this story from the Australian adding that no person was struck by any of the Skylab reentry relics.

312. Which planet other than Earth was the first to be studied by a satellite launched from Earth?

Venus. In 1967 the Soviet Venera 4 transmitted atmospheric data from Venus.

313. What piece of space clothing was the first to be lost in space?

A suit glove outer cover (thermal cover) lost by astronaut Ed White on the first U.S. space-walk (Gemini 4, June 3, 1965).

314. Who was referred to as the first cowboy in space?

Gemini 11 astronaut Dick Gordon. He "straddled" the Agena docking target spacecraft like a bronco bustin' cowboy to hold himself in position while on a space-walk to recover sample plates from the side of the Agena spacecraft.

315. Who controlled the TV camera (from Mission Control in Houston) to provide coverage of lift-offs (launches) of the last three Lunar Modules from the Moon (Apollo 15, 16, and 17)?

Communications Flight Controller, Ed Fendell. He had to allow for lag in radio signals. *See Q 482, 484.*

316. What spacecraft was dubbed the angry alligator?

The Agena docking target for Gemini 9. The launch shroud enclosing the docking end of the Agena opened only partway and looked like a set of open jaws that reminded Tom Stafford and Gene Cernan of an angry alligator.

317. According to their psychologist, what one thing did the first seven astronauts fear?

That something would prevent them from flying their mission when their time came.

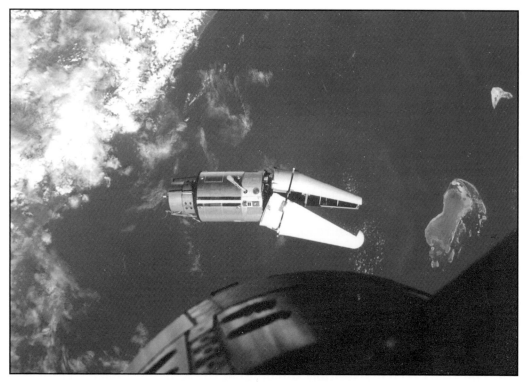

Photo of "angry alligator". *See Q 316*

318. Which astronaut worked for the Peace Corps after leaving NASA?

Donn F. Eisele (Apollo 7). After leaving NASA Donn was Director of the Peace Corps in Thailand.

319. Which Apollo astronaut was elected to the U.S. House of Representatives but died before serving as congressman?

John L. (Jack) Swigert, Jr. (Apollo 13). Jack was elected to the House (Colorado, 1982), but succumbed to cancer in December before serving.

320. Which NASA Mission Control Flight Director wore a "lucky" red vest?

Eugene F. (Gene) Kranz.

321. Which spacecraft crashed into the Moon while Armstrong and Aldrin were on the lunar surface?

The Soviet Luna 15. It hit the Moon 500 miles from their location two hours before the Apollo 11 liftoff from the lunar surface.

322. During the 1960s and 70s what local Texas wildlife posed occasional traffic hazards to astronauts as they taxied their T-38 jet aircraft at Ellington Air Force Base near the Johnson Space Center?

Deer, wolves and alligators. In one instance a deer was hit by a T-38 just after landing.

InfoNote: The biggest hazard of all was the Texas Prairie Chicken because they posed a risk to airborne aircraft. If hit in flight these critters could cause engine failure or smash in the lightweight windshield of the T-38s used by the astronauts. NASA's chief pilot, Joe Algranti, was at his wit's end until someone had an inspiration. The Texas Parks and Wildlife Department was contacted and they were instrumental in an effort to relocate the fowl.

The bottom of a Bell 47-G chopper was outfitted with wire mesh screen held by a tubular frame that nearly touched the ground and it was used to trap the birds. Then they were transferred to cages and moved to a safer home. That was over thirty years ago and there has been no recurrence of the problem.

323. What was the first spacecraft (from Earth) to lift off the surface of an extraterrestrial body?

The U.S. Surveyor 6, 1967. After landing on the Moon and performing initial investigations, it restarted its engine and moved to a new site for additional photographs.

324. The VAB (Vehicle Assembly Building) at the Kennedy Space Center was designed to withstand hurricane force winds of what strength or velocity?

125 miles per hour.

325. What was the first man-made object to strike the Moon?

The Soviet spacecraft Luna 2 in September 1959.

326. Who was the first Japanese astronaut to make a space-walk?

Takao Doi. On Shuttle mission STS-87. Doi performed two EVAs for a total of 12hrs. 44min.

327. Who was the first Payload Specialist (non-NASA astronaut) to make three Shuttle flights?

Charles D. (Charlie) Walker, sponsored by the McDonnell Douglas Company, was on the crew of Shuttle missions 41D (September 1984), 51D (April 1985) and 61B (November-December 1985). Charlie also has the record for the most frequent space flights, three flights in fifteen months. *See Q 19 sidebar*, **Titles for Spacefarers**.

328. Is the Great Wall of China visible to the unaided eye from low Earth orbit?

No. This is one of those popular fallacies that seems to live on and on. Some have even asserted it can be seen from the Moon! *See sidebar,* **Popular Fallacies.**

329. What family trait did the first two groups of astronauts share in common?

They were eldest sons in their families.

330. Which mission was the first to require a three-shift operation of the Houston Mission Control Center?

Gemini 4.

331. What company built the giant crawler-transporter (CT) that transports Shuttle to the launch pad?

The Marion Power Shovel Company of Marion, Ohio. Two were built in 1965 to transport the Saturn rockets to the pad and now they do the same for the Shuttle. They are the largest "tracked" land vehicles in the world. The empty weight of the CT is six million pounds and it is 131 feet long, 114 feet wide, 20 feet high with a 90-foot square deck for mounting the mobile launcher and Shuttle.

332. What company offers to take into space the cremation ashes of people?

Celestis, Inc. of Houston, TX. The fee is $4,800 for a ¼-ounce capsule of an individual's remains.

333. What did ALT stand for in the Shuttle program?

Approach and Landing Tests (The Enterprise glide tests to Edwards AFB, California).
See Q 12 and Q 227.

334. Who were the first cosmonauts to enter an American spacecraft (in space)?

Cosmonauts Alexei Leonov and Valeri Kubasov, during the Apollo-Soyuz joint mission.

Popular Fallacies

The following are the six most popular and enduring misconceptions about space flight.

1. **Fallacy**: NASA has a special room where they can cancel gravity and make things float.
Truth: People viewing scenes photographed in the zero-g aircraft (Q 250) have assumed they occurred in a special NASA ground facility.

2. **Fallacy:** Astronauts are really slammed back at lift-off.
Truth: Lift-off forces are relatively light (About 1.1 to 1.2 g's for the Saturn and a hefty 1.6 g's for the Shuttle). The highest forces are felt at the end of first stage boost as the launch vehicle gets lighter (about four g's for Saturn rockets). The Shuttle engines are throttled to keep forces under three g's.

3. **Fallacy:** The Great Wall of China is the man-made feature most easily seen from Earth orbit.
Truth: It can't be seen with the naked eye. However, large airfields and agricultural fields can be seen quite easily.

4. **Fallacy:** Astronauts make a lot of money and get extra pay for making a flight.
Truth: The average astronaut pay is about the same as for a Registered Nurse and no flight bonuses are paid. However, it is true that cosmonauts usually receive flight bonuses and may get performance bonuses as well. *See Q 692 for pay offered to first astronauts selected.*

5. **Fallacy:** Astronauts have to carry passports.
Truth: No passports are necessary. In the Astronaut Rescue Agreement of 1968 signatory nations agreed to provide the safe return of astronauts or cosmonauts who happen to make an emergency landing in their country. *See Q 284.*

6. **Fallacy:** Astronauts who landed on the Moon had suicide pills to use if they couldn't launch back to lunar orbit.
Truth: Not so! A quick and painless way to go would be to depressurize the spacecraft.

335. Who built the Spacelab, a scientific laboratory carried in the Shuttle payload bay?

The European Space Agency (ESA).

336. What was the largest pressurized compartment (single, open, continuous volume, without partitions) ever used in a manned spacecraft?

The Forward Compartment of Skylab's Orbital Workshop. It was a domed cylinder 21 feet in diameter and 23 feet long and accounted for half of Skylab's pressurized (habitable) volume. *See Q 214.*

337. How did American prisoners of war (POWs) in Viet Nam (subjected to news blackout) learn that NASA had made a successful lunar landing?

A graphic on a sugar packet in a Red Cross shipment depicted the Apollo 11 crew and Lunar Module on the Moon (personal communication from a friend who was a POW in Hanoi).

338. Which Mercury Astronaut used the Call Sign, Aurora 7?

Scott M. (Scotty) Carpenter.

339. Who logged the most space walk time for women astronauts in the 20th century?

Kathryn C. (Kathy or K.T.) Thornton. She logged over 21 hours on three space-walks.

340. When was the last Saturn V used to launch a payload?

May 14, 1973. On this date it launched the Skylab space station (unmanned).

341. Which Shuttle was the only one to be fitted with ejection seats?

Columbia. The two ejection seats were removed after the fourth Shuttle mission.

342. How were hair clippings collected during haircuts aboard Skylab?

By vacuum flow. A special screen/vacuum was provided in the ceiling of the bathroom to collect the hair. Some crews used the Skylab vacuum cleaner to collect the hair.

343. Who took the first photographs of the Earth from space?

John Glenn, during the third Mercury manned mission.

344. What caused the death of the crew during their return from the Soviet space station, Salyut 1?

A jolt from explosive bolts used to jettison their service module opened a ventilation valve and dumped the air from the reentry spacecraft module. This occurred prior to reentry but the valve was supposed to have been opened just before landing. The spacecraft made an automatic reentry and landing and it wasn't until recovery crews opened the hatch that the tragedy was discovered.

345. Who was the first crewman to lose a camera in space?

Mike Collins, Gemini 10, during a space-walk to the Agena rendezvous target vehicle.

346. When was the first double rendezvous accomplished in space?

July 1966. On Gemini 10 Young and Collins first rendezvoused with their primary Gemini 10 Agena target and later with the Gemini 8 Agena target.

347. Who was the first person to do three spacewalks (EVAs) during a single space flight?

Buzz Aldrin (Gemini 12, November 1966). Two were "stand-up" EVAs with Buzz operating from the open hatch of the spacecraft. Shuttle Astronaut Pierre Thuot was the first to do three spacewalks independent of the mother ship (STS-49, May 1992). See Q 219.

348. Who was the first person to transfer to another spacecraft in orbit?

Mike Collins, Gemini 10, transferred to the Agena target vehicle to recover sample collectors.

349. Who set the Moon land speed record with the Lunar Roving Vehicle (LRV)?

John Young, Apollo 16. During performance tests, he reached a speed of 11 mph. (17.7 kph.)

350. Who was the last person to set foot (step down) on the Moon during the 20th century?

Dr. Harrison H. (Jack) Schmitt, Apollo 17, December 1972.

351. Which satellite caused radioactive contamination when it crashed in Canada?

John Young driving the LRV on the Moon. *See Q 349.*

Soviet Cosmos 954 (January 1978).

352. What aircraft did the first seven astronauts use for flight proficiency training?

The U.S. Air Force F-106.

353. Who was the first NASA administrator?

Dr. T. Keith Glennan, former president of the Case Institute of Technology.

354. When was the public first exposed to the backward countdown sequence to ignition for a rocket launch?

In 1928. It was included in the script of a German Science Fiction film, Woman On the Moon. Hermann Oberth of the VfR (the German Society for Space Travel) was scientific advisor for the film.

355. What satellite was first to fly past another planet?

The U.S. Mariner 2. It made a fly-by of Venus, December, 14, 1962.

356. What was the name of NASA's Florida launch facility before it was named the Kennedy Space Center?

Launch Operations Center (LOC). See Q 431.

357. What does the acronym HHMU stand for?

Hand Held Maneuvering Unit. The HHMU was used by Gemini EVA astronauts White and Collins in the 60s, tested aboard (inside) Skylab in the 70s, and again by Shuttle EVA astronauts in the 90s.

358. How many people watched the Apollo 11 astronauts explore the Moon's surface?

It is estimated that 1/5 of the World's population (500 million) watched the live TV coverage. Count it correct if you said anything between 400 and 500 million.

359. What space food was served to dinner guests of the president of McDonnell Aircraft (builder of the Mercury and Gemini spacecraft)?

Banana pellets. They were used as performance rewards during the training of chimpanzees and also during the chimps' Mercury test flights. After the chimp flights were concluded the pellets became surplus so the frugal Scotsman, Mr. McDonnell, made good use of them.

360. Which U.S. space mission is sometimes referred to as Apollo 18?

The Apollo portion of the Apollo-Soyuz joint U. S. -Soviet space mission.

361. Where were the first seven astronauts based when they joined NASA?

At the Langley Flight Research Center near Norfolk, Virginia.

362. Which spacecraft was the first to make two manned flights into space?

Shuttle Columbia.

363. Which Apollo astronaut was once a Smoke Jumper for the U.S. Department of Interior?

Stuart A. (Stu) Roosa (Apollo 14). He served with a team who parachuted into areas to fight forest fires. Between his freshman and sophomore college years Stu made 12 jumps to fight fires in Montana and Oregon.

364. Who were the first astronauts to have food condiments available?

Skylab 3 (second manned visit). The first Skylab crew recommended addition of condiments. Liquid pepper, hot sauce, liquid salt, horseradish, garlic and ketchup were included. See Q 777.

Confusion Reigns

When the Skylab crews were announced in 1971 the prime crews set about designing their mission insignia or "patch" as it was usually called. The missions were officially designated as:

Skylab 1: for the unmanned launch of the Skylab space station on a giant Saturn V, and Skylab 2, 3 and 4 for the manned visits, which were lofted to space by Saturn 1B rockets.

That seemed simple enough but mischief was not long in coming. We began receiving flight procedures documents (check lists and other training materials) labeled SLM-1, SLM-2 and SLM-3 (Skylab Manned Mission 1, 2 and 3). Other documents were labeled SL-2, SL-3 and SL-4 (conforming to the official mission designations). It became a confusing mess because we began receiving mail and other documents clearly meant for one of the other crews, and the people in the Astronaut Office mailroom became as bewildered, perplexed and uncertain as the rest of us.

In the meantime we had designed our mission patches incorporating the official numeric designations (Skylab 2, 3, and 4). During a visit by the NASA Headquarters Director of the Skylab Program, Pete Conrad asked him, "Are we 1, 2 and 3 or are we 2, 3 and 4"? He said, "you are 1, 2 and 3". All of us went back to work and designed new patches to incorporate the numerals 1, 2 and 3. Skylab 1 and 2 used Roman numerals and Jerry, Ed and I used the Arabic numeral 3. The designs were rendered by artists and sent to NASA Headquarters for approval. The whole process took several months, and the artwork didn't arrive at NASA Headquarters until about six months before the scheduled launch of the Skylab.

The Associate Administrator for

365. What living creatures were the first passengers on a balloon flight?

A sheep, a rooster and a duck, September 19, 1783 near the Palace of Versailles outside Paris, France.

366. Who was the first Shuttle Commander to land on a concrete runway?

Thomas K. (Ken or T.K.) Mattingly, at the completion of STS-4 (fourth flight of Columbia), July 4, 1982, at Edwards Air Force Base, California. Prior flights had landed on dry lakebeds, two at Edwards and one at the White Sands backup strip near Alamogordo, New Mexico. *See Q 211.*

367. Which satellite was the first to transmit global cloud coverage photographs?

Tiros, launched April 1, 1960. During its life it transmitted 22,500 pictures from an altitude of 450 miles above the Earth.

Crazy Quote: *When asked by Arthur C. Clarke to present a paper on the meteorological uses of satellites (weather satellites) the response was, " ... they would be of very little value."* Dr. Harry Waxler, chief of research of the U. S. Weather Bureau, 1954.

368. Why did the numbering of the Skylab missions cause so much confusion?

Manned visits were officially named Skylab 2, 3 and 4, but many called them Skylab 1, 2 and 3. *See sidebar,* **Confusion Reigns**.

369. Who was the first person to use underwater suited training to prepare for his space-walks?

Mike Collins, during training for Gemini 10, July 1966.

370. Who was the first Japanese astronaut to fly in space as a crewmember?

Mamoru Mohri (STS-47, September 1992).

371. Which spacecraft was the first to provide separate private sleep compartments for the crew?

Skylab. Each crewman had a compartment roughly the size of a telephone booth (80 cu. ft.).

372. Which spacecraft was the first to transmit a close-up picture of the surface of Mars?

Viking, July 1976.

373. During what space flight did NASA begin preparations to launch a rescue mission?

Skylab 3 (second mission, July - September 1973).

InfoNote: Fuel (propellant) leaks were detected in the attitude control rocket system of the Apollo Service Module, which could have prevented a successful return. After careful evaluation ground technicians determined that the leaks were less serious than originally thought. The rescue mission was scheduled for early September but never launched. Skylab 3 executed a safe return using special work-around procedures developed by Mission Control.

374. What mementos did the Apollo 11 crew leave on the Moon to honor deceased spacemen?

An Apollo 1 shoulder patch to honor astronauts Grissom, White and Chaffee who died in the Apollo 1 spacecraft fire during ground tests (January 1967), and medals given by the widows of cosmonauts Gagarin and Komarov. See Q 288, 289.

375. After returning from the first Moon landing, what peculiar precautionary health procedure was performed just after the

*(**Confusion Reigns:** continued)*

Manned Space Flight took one look at the artwork and disapproved the design because he said the official flight designations, "2, 3 and 4" were to be used. Thus informed, we dug out our original designs (for 2, 3 and 4) and were in the process of getting the artwork done when informed by Headquarters "not to bother". We could use the designs for 1, 2 and 3. Then we found out why.

The people who had manufactured the Skylab flight clothing (to be worn onboard) had already completed their work several weeks earlier in order to get the clothes packaged and shipped to the Cape to meet their deadline (for stowage onboard Skylab which was already in pre-launch processing).

Furthermore, they had already used the designs submitted earlier for the mission patches. They didn't have time to wait for official approval. The designs using the numeric designation 1, 2 and 3 became approved by default because items with these patches were already stowed in the Skylab lockers at the Cape. Removing them for patch change-out was considered to be much too expensive and disruptive of launch preparations.

So, although officially designated as Skylab 2, 3 and 4, the mission insignias bear the numeric designations as follows: Skylab 2 (Roman numeral I), Skylab 3 (Roman numeral II) and Skylab 4 (Arabic numeral 3). When traveling in Afghanistan in 1975, I presented some Afghan VIPs with our Skylab 4 mission patch. One lady looked thoroughly confused and asked about the numeral 3 on the Skylab 4 patch. I gave her this long-winded explanation and, by the time I finished, the Afghans were roaring with laughter.

This has to be the most exasperating bit of space trivia ever, and it is

(**Confusion Reigns:** continued)
especially confusing to autograph collectors who still scratch their heads trying to sort out their trophies. On the bright side, the Skylab missions set successive space endurance records of 28, 59 and 84 days.

Skylab 2 emblem.

Skylab 3 emblem.

Skylab 4 emblem.

Apollo 11 astronauts walked from the recovery helicopter to the quarantine van on the aircraft carrier?

A NASA scientist sprayed disinfectant along the path where the crew had walked.
See Q 500.

376. What were the first living creatures launched from Cape Canaveral and recovered alive?

Two Rhesus monkeys named Able and Baker. They were launched on May 28, 1959 aboard a Jupiter missile, which reached an altitude of 300 miles and traveled 1,500 miles across the Atlantic. Able and Baker lived out their lives in a special habitat at the U.S. Space and Rocket Center, Huntsville, AL.

377. Which astronaut was (is) buried in China?

Dr. Karl G. Henize. He is buried at the base camp on Mt. Everest. See Q 94.

378. What finger pains were reported by Apollo-era astronauts following long space-walks?

Sore fingernails. Extensive manipulative tasks (with suit gloves) tended to lift up on the fingernails and the soreness lasted for several days after their space walks.

379. What is the name of Russia's counterpart to NASA?

In the U.S. it's called the Russian Space Agency (RSA). In Russia it's called Rosavia Cosmos or Rosavia Kosmos (Russian Aeronautics [also Aviation] and Space Agency).

380. Who was the first ex-professional athlete to go into space?

Shuttle Mission Specialist Manly L. (Sonny) Carter. He played for the Atlanta Chiefs of the North

American Soccer League before he was selected as an astronaut.

381. Who was the youngest person ever selected as a U. S. astronaut (in the 20th century)?

Anthony W. (Tony) England. Tony was an outstanding geologist and geophysicist and joined the astronaut corps when he was only 25. Tony was in the sixth group (second scientist astronaut selection) in 1967, and flew on Shuttle mission 51F in July 1985.

382. The 1996 astronaut selection included two people named Kelly. What is their relationship?

They are twin brothers, Mark and Scott. This was the first time ever that siblings joined the astronaut corps.

383. Who was the first foreign citizen to fly as a crewmember on a U. S. spacecraft?

Ulf Merbold, from Germany, flew on Shuttle mission STS-9 (first Spacelab mission-November 1983).

384. Who was the first astronaut to grow a full beard while in space?

Jerry Carr, final Skylab mission commander (November 1983-February 1984).

385. What tool did the first Skylab crew use to cut free a solar wing boom that failed to extend and deploy?

A cable cutter (similar to pruning shears). Pete Conrad and Joe Kerwin cut a strap of metal wrapped around the assembly and it sprung free, permitting deployment of a much-needed solar power array. *See Q 285 and sidebar,* **Whoops!**

386. Who was the first astronaut to return to military service after serving with NASA?

Whoops!

When a meteoroid debris shield ripped loose a minute after launch of the Skylab space station it tore off one entire solar wing and jammed the other one, preventing deployment of the boom holding the solar arrays. The first Skylab crew launched and docked with the Skylab about a week later carrying with them tools for fixing the problem. After preparing for a space walk Pete and Joe worked their way back along the Skylab and got into position to cut the metal strap holding the boom. It wasn't any easy task because there were no handholds or foot restraints. Joe helped steady Pete and he cut through the strap with the cable cutters.

The boom, under force from a compressed air piston, suddenly swung out from the side of Skylab hurling Joe and Pete out into space to the end of their suit hoses (umbilicals). They reeled themselves back in by pulling on their umbilicals and the job was done. They commented later that they were grateful that no one at mission control could see their "swan dive" into space or someone on the ground would have had a heart attack. In effect, Pete and Joe saved a $2.5 billion program.

Photo of the bolt cutters.

Buzz Aldrin. He became commandant of the U.S.A. F. Test Pilots School at Edwards AFB, California.

387. During the Apollo program which astronaut office secretary was nicknamed Charlie?

Charlotte Ober.

388. Who was the photographer that documented the survival training and field trips of Mercury, Gemini, Apollo-era and Shuttle astronauts?

Andrew E. (Pat) Patneski.

389. Which NASA field center controlled the study of the Mars surface by the robot Sojourner (1998)?

JPL (Jet Propulsion Laboratory), Pasadena, California.

390. While traveling to and from the Moon what was the name of the maneuver Apollo astronauts used to equalize Sun-side heating (and dark-side chilling) of the spacecraft?

Barbecue Mode. It was a slow roll (rotation) that exposed all outside surfaces to sunlight for half of each roll. If held at a fixed attitude one side of the spacecraft got too hot and the other side too cold.

391. How long does it take to fly from Earth to Mars (or Mars to Earth)?

Approximately nine months. However, an eighteen-month wait is required before starting back.

392. Who was the first director of the Manned Spacecraft Center (now the Johnson Space Center)?

Dr. Robert R. Gilruth. *See Q 89.*

393. At the Johnson Space Center Mission Control Center, what Flight Controller is called FIDO?

The Flight Dynamics Officer. FIDO is responsible for targeting (planning) all engine burns (thrusting maneuvers).

394. What weather event caused a power failure at the Russian Mission Control Center (July 8, 1999)?

A severe hailstorm. Part of the Center was without power for over five hours.

395. Who piloted the first successful sustained flight of an airplane, Orville or Wilbur Wright?

Orville. His brother Wilbur ran alongside the aircraft, which took off into a 27 mile per hour headwind.

Crazy Quote: *In response to a friend's prediction that men would eventually be able to fly in heavier-than-air machines, a minister said, "Flying is reserved for the angels. I beg you not mention that again lest you be guilty of blasphemy." Rev. Milton Wright, 1870 (father of Orville and Wilbur).*

396. What is the name of the rock and roll band whose players are all astronauts?

Max Q. *See Q 608 for an explanation of Max Q.*

397. Who was the first African American woman to fly in space?

Mae C. Jemison. She flew on STS-47 in September 1992.

398. Who was the first person to fly around the Statue of Liberty?

Wilbur Wright in 1908. It was a public relations stunt to show off an aircraft's capability.

399. From Mercury through the Apollo era, suited-astronauts carried a suitcase-shaped device on their trip to the launch pad. What did it contain?

Breathing oxygen. The portable air conditioner supplied oxygen to the crewmen from the time they finished suiting up until they hooked in to the spacecraft supply.

400. What trainer used for the Mercury astronauts was described as the "ultimate in wild carnival rides"?

The MASTIF (Multiple Axis Space Test Inertia Facility). It was built at the Lewis Research Center, Cleveland, Ohio to condition astronauts to wild tumbles they might encounter in space. MASTIF was also called a "maniacal carrousel." Wally Schirra referred to the MASTIF as an "instrument of torture."

401. Who was the first woman to be Commander of a Shuttle flight?

Eileen Collins. She was Commander of STS-93 flown in July 1999.

402. Where was an Apollo Moon rock first put on public display?

At the Smithsonian Air and Space museum in October 1969. The rock was brought back from the Moon by the Apollo 11 crew (July 1969).

403. While in Star City, Apollo-Soyuz support crewman Bob Overmyer adjusted the position of his chair, ripped the carpet and revealed what electronic device?

A microphone (bug). Bob stated later that he thought it was more for keeping tabs on the cosmonauts rather than spying on the astronauts. Both the cosmonauts and astronauts had a good laugh from the incident.

404. What was the name of the first satellite launched from Sea Launch, an ocean-based platform?

DirecTVR (9 October 1999). It was the first commercial launch from their floating platform, which uses a location south of Hawaii near the equator.

405. Which astronaut was first to address a joint session of Congress?

John Glenn, following his orbital flight in Friendship 7.

406. Who was the first member of royalty to fly in space?

Prince Sultan Al-Saud, of Saudi Arabia (Shuttle mission 51G June 1985).

407. What was the first animal to die in space?

Laika, a Russian dog aboard Sputnik 2, November 5 or 6, 1957. *See Q 1.*

InfoNote: Although there was enough food and life support for seven days Laika died after the cabin temperature soared to 40° C (104° F). It was thought that external insulation on the Sputnik II had been torn away during incomplete separation from the booster rocket's upper stage, allowing the cabin temperature to increase to unsafe levels.

408. At what facility were the Shuttle Orbiters assembled and delivered to NASA?

At the Rockwell plant in Palmdale, California.

409. Who was the first astronaut selected from the U.S. Coast Guard?

Bruce E. Melnick, selected in 1988, flew on Shuttle missions STS-41 (1990) and STS-49 (1992).

410. Which astronaut served with NASA for the longest time during the 20th century?

John W. Young. John had served NASA over 37 years as of 1 January 2000.

411. Which astronaut guided the design of a new wristwatch for use in space?

Tom Stafford. It's called the Speedmaster Professional X-33 or the Omega Mars Watch.

412. Who was the only geologist to land on the Moon?

Harrison H. (Jack) Schmitt, on Apollo 17 December 1972.

413. How many LRVs (Lunar Roving Vehicles) are left on the Moon?

Three, from the last three Apollo missions, Apollo 15, 16 and 17.

414. In what year did Charles Lindbergh fly the Atlantic non-stop (New York to Paris)?

1927.

Crazy Quote: *After carefully studying Lindbergh's plane an aviation enthusiast said, "This fellow will never make it. He's doomed." Harry Guggenheim, millionaire philanthropist. It should be noted that, later on, Mr. Guggenheim and Lindbergh collaborated on many aeronautical technological efforts, including support for Dr. Goddard's rocket experiments.*

415. What religious ceremony had to be modified for the first Moslem astronaut, Saudi Prince Al-Saud (Shuttle mission 51G, June 1985)?

The five daily prayers facing Mecca and the ritual hand washing. Hand washing posed no problem but "facing Mecca" did! After consulting Moslem holy men, the number of prayers was reduced to three, during which he was merely required to face the Earth (a reasonable and sensible decision because Mecca's position would be continually changing with Shuttle orbital motion). Note: Obtaining approval from the holy men was especially important because 51G was flown during Ramadan, the holiest month of the Moslem year. The Prince fasted during his first day in orbit in observance of Ramadan.

416. Who was the first person to record a prayer in space?

Gordon Cooper aboard Faith 7, May 16, 1963. He recorded the prayer on the spacecraft tape recorder.

417. How did Skylab astronauts salt their food?

Salt water was squirted on the food using a device similar to a hypodermic syringe.

418. Who was the first passenger to fly in a powered aircraft?

Henry Farman flown by Leon De Lagrange, March 28, 1908 at Issy-les-Moulineaux, France.

419. What private corporation is responsible for preparing the Shuttle for launch?

The United Space Alliance (USA).

420. What was the name of the first simulator used to teach instrument flying in the U.S. Army Air Corps?

The Link Trainer. Originally, instrument flying was called "blind flying".

421. Who was the training officer for the first seven astronauts?

Robert Voas, a NASA psychologist.

422. Who built the first passenger jet aircraft for airline use?

The British De Havilland company. They manufactured the four-engine Comet used by the British Overseas Airways Corporation (BOAC).

Pitiful Prophecies: *"The aeroplane ... is not capable of unlimited magnification. It is not likely that it will ever carry more than five or seven passengers." Scientific American, June 1913.*

"Propulsion by the reaction of a simple jet cannot compete, in any respect, with airscrew (propeller) propulsion at such flying speeds as are now in prospect." Edward Buckingham, U. S. Bureau of Standards, 1923. Parenthesis added.

423. What unmanned spacecraft was the first to complete two space flights?

The Gemini II (Roman numeral for 2) spacecraft, built to qualify heat shields for the Department of Defense Manned Orbiting Laboratory (MOL) program, later canceled. Gemini II flew on 1 January 1965 and, after refurbishment, again on 2 November 1966.

424. Who was Al Shepard's secretary when he was Chief of the Astronaut Office?

Gay Alford.

425. Who made the first free flight of a helicopter?

Paul Cornu, a French inventor of the craft (November 13, 1907).

426. Which Mercury astronaut fell asleep during the countdown to his launch?

Gordon Cooper, during a delay in the countdown to the launch of Faith 7. (Cosmonaut Gherman Titov was the first person to sleep in space (Vostok 2, August 11, 1961).

427. Why did mission planners want to shave all the body hair off the Apollo 7 astronauts?

To reduce the risk of fire. Apollo 7 Commander Wally Schirra refused, saying, "If the danger is such that hair is a hazard, I would rather not fly the machine after all." NASA relented.

428. Who was director of the Moorhead Planetarium at the University of North Carolina, and acted as astronomy instructor for Apollo crews?

Tony Genzano.

429. What was contained in a special rations kit, placed in Wally Schirra's Mercury spacecraft by Wally's backup, Gordon Cooper?

A steak sandwich, a two-ounce bottle of Scotch and five cigarettes. It was merely a symbolic gesture because they were inaccessible to Wally.

430. What slip-up occurred as President Kennedy was awarding the Distinguished Service Medal to Al Shepard?

The President dropped the medal on the Whitehouse lawn.

431. Which is the correct name for the "Cape," Cape Canaveral or Cape Kennedy?

Cape Canaveral.

InfoNote: In the aftermath of President Kennedy's assassination (1963), the name of NASA's Florida launch facility (Launch Operations Center) as well as the coastline geographic feature (Cape Canaveral) were changed to honor the fallen leader. President Lyndon Johnson announced the renaming of Cape Canaveral to Cape Kennedy on Thanksgiving Day 1963. In the heyday of Apollo all launches were datelined from "Cape Kennedy".
The residents of Central Florida had objected to the renaming of a geographic feature which dated back to the 16th century and, in 1973, it was renamed Cape Canaveral by the U. S. Congress. The Kennedy Space Center (KSC) is located on Merritt Island and all Shuttles launch from Pads 39A or 39B at KSC. The Cape Canaveral Air Force Station is located on the strip of coastal land called Cape Canaveral.

432. What was the name of the prize Lindbergh won by making his solo flight across the Atlantic?

The Orteig Prize. Raymond Orteig put up $25,000 for the first non-stop flight from New York to Paris.

Early Breakthrough

Early Egyptian astronomers were obsessed with developing an accurate calendar to enable them to predict the annual flood of the Nile with greater accuracy. The flood occurred roughly in the second week of July (in our calendar) each year. The breakthrough came when they discovered that they could observe the rise of Sirius coincidental with the breaking of the top of the Sun's disk at the horizon (sunrise).

This event occurred precisely at the same position in the Earth's orbit around the Sun (same day of the year). This discovery enabled them to calibrate their calendar. Sirius is called the "dog star" because canus major (its constellation) is Latin for dog. The "dog days" of summer (July - August) occur when the "dog star" is near the Sun.

433. Which space traveler who made an orbital flight logged the least amount of time in space?

Cosmonaut Yuri Gagarin (One hour and forty-nine minutes).

434. Who performed the last space walk of the Apollo (lunar) program?

Ron Evans, Apollo 17.

435. Which Shuttle astronaut rang the opening bell at the New York Stock Exchange (January 7, 2000)?

Colonel Eileen Collins. On that day the Dow Jones Industrial Average rose 269 points.

436. Who was the nurse in Flight Medicine (Astronaut Clinic) during the first two decades of the Shuttle program?

Claudette Gage. See Q 146.

437. Which spacecraft was the first to host nine space walks?

Skylab. Nine were performed from the Skylab Airlock Module and one was a stand-up EVA performed from the Apollo Command Module hatch by Paul Weitz to assess the damage that occurred during the launch of the Skylab space station.

438. Why are most launches toward the east?

To get a free boost from the Earth's rotation. It's greatest at the equator (1,500 ft/sec - a bit over 1,000 mph); at Cape Canaveral in Florida (28½° N. latitude) it's dropped off to 1300 ft/sec or 885 mph. See Q 475, 593.

439. What is the brightest star in the sky (excluding our Sun and novas)?

Sirius, sometimes called the dog star (Constellation Canus Major). *See sidebar,* **Early Breakthrough**.

440. What is the mass of the Moon as compared to the Earth (in percentage) ?

About 1.23 % of the Earth's mass.

441. What was the duration of Al Shepard's Mercury flight?

15 minutes (including five minutes of weightlessness).

442. What is the length of the Shuttle payload bay?

60 feet. At 60' X 15', the payload bay is just less than 1/3 the size of a tennis court.

443. What is the inclination angle (for an Earth orbit)?

The angle the orbit plane makes with the equator where it crosses the equator moving northward. The angle is measured counterclockwise from the equatorial plane to the plane of the spacecraft's orbit. The maximum latitude of the orbit (north and south) is equal to the inclination angle. *See figure 1.*

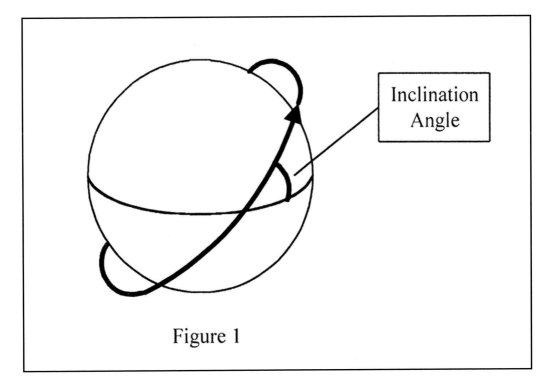

Inclination Angle

Figure 1

444. Where are the Shuttle's speed brakes located?

They are incorporated into the rudder (tail). The rudder "splits" to extend outward to the left and right to create extra drag when it's needed. An early rudder design of the X-15 proposed this capability.

445. What is the name of the fire-resistant material used as the outer layer of space suits?

Beta cloth, a Teflon-coated fiberglass fabric.

446. A spacecraft trajectory change from a lower orbit to a higher orbit is called what?

A transfer orbit (ditto for going from higher to lower).

447. At what altitude above the Earth is the ozone layer?

It extends from 10 to 20 miles above the surface.

448. How does the length of Valles Marineris, the vast gorge on Mars, compare with the Grand Canyon of Arizona?

It's about 15 times the length of the Grand Canyon. Valles Marineris (over 2500 miles long) would span the entire continent of North America (e.g. San Francisco, California to Cape Hatteras, North Carolina).

449. How did Skylab generate electrical power?

Power was provided from large solar arrays (solar cells) during the dayside of the orbit. Part of the power was used to charge batteries to provide power for the night-side of the orbit. The International Space Station has a similar system but with much greater capacity.

450. What special garment did the first lunar landing crew have to put on before getting out of their spacecraft after splashdown?

The Biological Isolation Garment (BIG). The BIG was a full body suit enclosure designed to prevent exposing the Earth to any back-contamination from the Moon. See Q 451, 517, 518.

451. What household antiseptic was used to swab down the astronauts after they got into their rubber rafts following splashdown at the end of Apollo Moon landing missions 11, 12 and 14?

An iodine solution. It was used by a navy scuba diver, also in a BIG, to scrub the outside of the BIG worn by the astronauts. The astronauts returned the favor by scrubbing him down. The spacecraft received the same treatment before it was hoisted aboard the recovery vessel. See Q 450, Q 518.

452. How does the size of the Earth compare to the Great Red Spot on Jupiter?

Three Earth-size discs, edge-to-edge, would be just short of spanning the Spot, which is about 25,000 miles wide.

453. Which manned spacecraft was the first to provide steering (maneuvering capability to change flight path) during reentry?

Gemini. This capability was needed to assure Apollo crews returning from the Moon would be able to steer during reentry to follow the proper reentry path. Accurate targeting for the reentry corridor plus the steering capability were essential for a safe return. *See sidebar,* **Not Too Steep - Not Too Shallow**.

454. What is an Astronomical Unit (AU)?

An AU is the average distance of the Earth from the sun, approximately 93 million miles or 150 million kilometers. (Count it correct if you're within 2 million miles or 3 million km.)

455. The asteroid belt of our solar system lies between which two planets?

Mars and Jupiter. Because the asteroids are small the planets easily disturb their paths. Many asteroids' orbits take them well inside the Earth's orbital path. See Q 655, Q 656.

456. What was the name of the Moon-mapping satellite that discovered permanently shaded sites near the lunar poles, potentially capable of harboring water ice?

Clementine, a low-cost Department of Defense satellite.

457. What did Lunar Prospector (Moon-orbiting satellite) discover in 1998 that led scientists to believe there is water ice in the Moon's polar regions?

Not Too Steep - Not Too Shallow

The targeting accuracy required for an Apollo reentry was described by one NASA engineer as "trying to shoot the fuzz off a tennis ball at a hundred yards." For reentry through the Earth's atmosphere when returning from the Moon, the astronauts were aiming for a 27-mile-thick corridor (the fuzz), wherein the air was thick enough to assure capture yet thin enough to avoid burning up the spacecraft. Steering within this corridor permitted control of the drag level to follow the prescribed reentry profile (path).

An abundance of hydrogen. Some NASA scientists believe the hydrogen originates from water ice buried in the permanently shaded polar regions of the Moon (the bottoms of deep craters). Other scientists speculate the hydrogen comes from the solar wind. See Q 649.

458. What is the average distance from the Earth to the Moon?

239,000 miles (384,000 kilometers). Count it correct if you're within 5,000 mi. or 8,000 km).

459. At what altitude did the Apollo astronauts orbit the Moon?

At 60 - 70 miles (96 – 112 km) above the Moon's surface.

460. What material was used for the heat shields of Mercury, Gemini and Apollo spacecraft?

A silicon compound (chemically akin to pure sand) injected into the cells of a fiberglass honeycomb structure. See Q 726.

461. What term was used to describe the "wearing away" of the heat shield during reentry?

Ablation, the conversion of the solid to a gas. Ablation absorbs the enormous heat generated during entry.

462. Which spacecraft was the first to have an airlock as part of its primary structure?

Skylab. It accommodated two suited crewmen. The airlock for cosmonaut Leonov's space-walk (Voskhod 2) was an inflatable structure. For EVAs in Gemini and Apollo, the entire spacecraft had to be depressurized. See Q 206.

463. How much did the Mercury spacecraft weigh?

2,100 pounds.

464. Why is a geostationary orbit (at 22,320 miles) undesirable for a manned space station?

Any of the following are correct answers, bearing in mind current technology limitations.
(1) Ionizing radiation is excessive; this altitude would be within the upper radiation belt (trapped protons).
(2) Getting to this altitude (and back) would be expensive in terms of propellant required (would reduce the payload capability considerably).

(3) Earth studies would be adversely affected. The distance would reduce accuracy of observations (reduce resolution) and the stationary position would only permit observation of one part of the Earth. However, this could be an advantage if scientists wanted to make continuous long-term observations of a specific site or portion of the Earth. *See Table 2,* **Summary of Orbital Classifications,** *Q 472.*

465. What is a mascon, a term used to describe peculiar properties of the Moon's crust?

It stands for <u>mas</u>s <u>con</u>centration, presumed to be volcanic intrusions of greater density than surrounding surface crustal material. Mascons affect the trajectory of spacecraft orbiting the Moon causing slight variations (perturbations) in the orbital path. *See Q 722.*

466. Which planet in the solar system has the lowest density?

Saturn. Its average density is 7/10 that of water.

467. On which planet is the Great Rift Valley located?

Venus. It is over 150 miles wide and 1,400 miles long.

468. What emergency escape system is provided for Shuttle astronauts and pad crews if a problem occurs late in the launch countdown and they must abandon the launch pad?

Seven slide wire carriages. They are positioned at the White Room level on the launch service structure, each accommodating three people. Astronauts and/or pad workers get into the carriage, release it and slide down the wires to the ground 1,200 feet from the launch pad where they enter an underground haven. A braking system slows the carriages as they approach the ground.

Photo of the slide wire carriages.

469. What does NASA call an orbit in which a spacecraft awaits the next thrust phase of a planned mission?

A parking orbit.

470. What Earth orbital path is known as the Clarke Belt?

It's a path 22,320 miles (35,920 km) above the Earth's surface directly above the equator, where a satellite's orbital velocity equals the Earth's rotation rate (satellite appears stationary as viewed from the Earth). British physicist, mathematician and author, Arthur C. Clarke, first proposed this orbit path for use as a site for communications relay in 1945.

471. How is artificial gravity generated aboard a space vehicle?

By rotating the space assembly, which generates centrifugal force. For a given rotation rate, this force increases as distance from the center of rotation increases.

472. What is meant by the acronym GEO?

Geosynchronous Earth Orbit. For a GEO, the time to orbit equals the time for one complete Earth rotation. When the orbit is very nearly circular and equatorial (at 22,320 miles), it is also called a "geostationary orbit" because it appears stationary when viewed from the Earth's surface. See Table 2, **Summary of Orbital Classifications.**

Summary of Orbital Classifications	
LEO (Low Earth Orbit)	70 - 300 miles
MEO (Medium Earth Orbit)	300 - 22,320 miles
HEO (High Earth Orbit)	22,320 - 60,000 miles
PEO (Polar Earth Orbit)	Orbits that pass near the Earth's poles
GEO (Geosynchronous Earth Orbit)	Orbit whose period equals the Earth's rotation period*
Geostationary Orbit (22,320 mi.)	A GEO that appears stationary (as viewed from the Earth)
Sun Synchronous Orbit	Crosses the equator at the same local time of day each orbit
Parking Orbit	Usually a LEO from which transfer to a higher orbit is made
Transfer Orbit	A half-orbit that takes the spacecraft to a higher/lower orbit

* The Earth's rotational period is actually 23 hours, 56 minutes, 4 seconds but a GEO is usually referred to as a 24-hour orbit. 24-hour orbits do not have to be stationary nor circular but they do retrace the same path over the Earth (ground track) on each successive orbit.

Table 2

473. What is the Oort Cloud?

It is a band of solid objects beyond the Kuiper Belt (at the fringes of our solar system). When disturbed by the gravitational influence of other objects some are displaced, travel in toward the sun and become comets. These comets may never reappear in historic time spans. See Q 767.

474. Which spacecraft was the first to use fuel cells to generate electricity?

Gemini. These fuel cells combined hydrogen and oxygen and produced water in addition to electricity.

475. What is escape velocity from the Earth (approximately)?

25,000 mph (40,000 kph) or 7 miles per sec (11 kilometers per second). *See Q 438, 593.*

476. What was the longest American space flight prior to Skylab (1973-74)?

Gemini 7 (14 days, December 1967).

477. What is the South Atlantic Anomaly (SAA)?

The SAA is a low spot in the inner radiation belt around the Earth. The axis of the Earth's magnetic field does not pass through the center of the Earth and this offset causes the inner belt to sag lower over the southern Atlantic Ocean. Space-walks are scheduled to avoid passing through the SAA to avoid exposing crewmembers to the higher level of ionizing radiation that exists in this region. *See Q 635.*

478. The time or period for one low Earth orbit (say, at 200 miles altitude) is roughly 1½ hours. What is the approximate time for a low orbit around Mars?

Approximately 107 minutes or about 1¾ hour.

479. What is the peak g-force felt by Shuttle astronauts during reentry?

About one and one-half g's.

480. Why do Shuttle astronauts drink more fluids than normal just before de-orbit and reentry?

NASA physicians refer to this practice as "fluid loading." It increases the blood volume of the body, which aids in resisting light-headedness sometimes experienced during the 20-minute entry. During much of the entry the force is about 1½ g's, which tends to force blood away from the head toward the feet.

481. What was the Earth weight of the suit backpack (PLSS) used by Apollo Moon-walkers?

On Earth the backpack or Portable Life Support System (PLSS) weighed 190 pounds (85 kilograms). On the Moon the weight was about 35 pounds (15 kilograms).

482. How long does it take for radio signals to travel from Earth to Mars (one way) when Mars is closest to the Earth?

Approximately 4 1/3 minutes. When they're farthest apart (on opposite sides of the Sun) the time is about 21 minutes. *See Q 315.*

483. What did the acronym ARIA stand for during the Apollo program?

Apollo Range Instrumentation Aircraft. These were Air Force Boeing KC-135 refueling tanker jet aircraft fitted with seven-foot antennas in the nose to provide spacecraft tracking information to supplement data from ground and ship tracking sites.

Photo of the ARIA aircraft. *See Q 483.*

484. How long does it take for radio signals to travel from Earth to the Moon (and vice versa)?

1.28 seconds (approximately 1¼ seconds). *See Q 315.*

485. How does the gravity force on the Moon's surface compare with the Earth's?

Lunar surface gravity force is 1/6 of Earth's.

486. What is the diameter of the antennas in NASA's Deep Space Network (DSN)?

230 feet. Three are positioned around the world [Goldstone, California; Madrid, Spain and Canberra, Australia] to provide 2-way contact with spacecraft at great distances from Earth. Because of the approximate equidistant spacing one antenna will always have access to any given spot in the heavens.

487. How does the gravity force on Mars compare with the Earth's?

Mars surface gravity force is 1/3 of the Earth's.

488. It has been said, "Venus may be a good place to orbit but you wouldn't want to land there." Why?

We're talking instant barbecue of your carcass. The surface temperature is hot enough to melt lead (over 800° F/480° C) and the surface atmospheric pressure is 90 times Earth sea level pressure (and you thought angina was bad!).

489. Which crews were subjected to the highest deceleration (braking) forces during reentry: (a) Apollo crews returning from the Moon, or (b) the Mercury astronauts?

(b) the Mercury astronauts. The average peak g-load of a Mercury reentry was higher (7.7 g's), whereas the highest g-load for Apollo astronauts was just under 7 g's. Al Shepard's peak g-force was 11.6 gs.

490. Shuttle mission 41D's main engines shut down on the pad after ignition because of damage to an integrated circuit (IC) in the spacecraft computer. What caused the IC to fail?

Human saliva (spit) contaminated the IC while it was being manufactured and potassium chloride (KCl) in the spit ate away part of the IC circuitry.

491. What's the difference between the terms _rev_ (revolution) and _orbit_ used to discuss flight paths around the Earth?

An _orbit_ is 360° of travel around the Earth, irrespective of the orbital direction. A _rev_ is the path traveled between successive crossings of the same meridian (line of longitude). For eastward orbits a _rev_ in low Earth orbit near the equator takes about 6 minutes longer (and 1,700 miles farther) than an _orbit_. This is because the Earth's rotation has moved the reference meridian to the east during the course of the spacecraft's path around the Earth.

492. What chemical is used to remove carbon dioxide from the Shuttle atmosphere?

Lithium hydroxide (LiOH).

493. Which space mission was the first to experiment with artificial gravity?

Gemini 11, September 1966. After Dick Gordon attached a 50-foot tether between the Gemini spacecraft and the Agena docking target, Pete Conrad established a slow rotation generating a low level of artificial gravity, as the two spacecraft rotated around at the end of the tether joining them.

The Velocity Paradox

The flight plan of Gemini 4 (Jim McDivitt and Ed White) called for an attempt to rendezvous with the second stage of the Titan booster that had just placed them into orbit. After reaching orbit Gemini 4 was trailing the second stage by about 100 yards so Jim McDivitt thrusted toward the spent stage, their rendezvous target. Failing to close in on the target Jim tried some more thrusts toward the target only to watch the target move farther away. The effort was finally abandoned but a good lesson was learned.

By thrusting toward the target ahead of them in orbit, the initial effect was a slight increase in velocity but the added energy caused their spacecraft to begin a slight climb and, as their path got higher, they started to slow down. The larger the orbit the slower the velocity is.

To catch up with a rendezvous target a slight thrust opposite the direction of travel is required. The initial effect is a slight decrease in velocity, which causes a descent and results in a higher velocity after a few minutes. This property of orbits leads to the apparent contradiction in terms which is usually stated as follows: **You have to slow down to speed up - and speed up to slow down.**

494. What scientist postulated the General Theory of Relativity?

Albert Einstein (1915).

495. When the Shuttle starts reentry, it is traveling at how many times the speed of sound?

About 25 times the speed of sound (or Mach 25). For some reentries, the Shuttle is moving close to Mach 26. The highest speed for spacecraft returning from Earth orbit occurs just before reentry drag build-up. *See sidebar*, **The Velocity Paradox**.

496. Who coined the term, astronautics, to describe the study of space flight?

Belgian science fiction author, J.J. Rosny (1927, during a dinner party in Paris).

497. What was the lift-off thrust of the Saturn 5 Moon rocket?

Seven and a half million pounds.

498. What facility was created to assure that all necessary crew equipment is onboard for Shuttle flights?

The Flight Equipment Processing Facility (called the FEPAC). Food, clothing, cameras, suits and other equipment are overseen by this group to assure a complete "shipset" will be onboard when the Shuttle launches. If this name, FEPAC, confuses you, join the club. The term FEPAC ("fee pack") comes from the name of the legal agreement (Flight Equipment Processing Contract) between NASA and the contractor that manages the Facility.

499. What is the name of the highest mountain on Mars?

Olympus Mons (Mount Olympus). It rises 13¾ miles (22 km) above surrounding plains and is over 340 miles (550 km) in diameter. By comparison, the summit of Mount Everest, the highest mountain on Earth, is 5 ½ miles (8.8 km) above sea level.

500. Why were Apollo crews placed in isolation (quarantine) after return from a lunar landing mission?

Fear of back-contamination (contamination of the Earth from the Moon). *See Q 375.*

InfoNote: Some reputable scientists had theorized that it was possible for the crewmen and space hardware to carry back dormant microorganisms such as mutated viruses or bacteria to which Earthlings would be vulnerable. After Apollo 14 (the last crew to be quarantined) there was no evidence to suggest even the slightest presence of such microorganisms so the procedure was discontinued. However, it is likely that similar precautions will be taken for spacecraft returning from Mars and other bodies in the solar system where there has been contact with alien surface materials.
Lest we be too critical of the scientists who insisted on the quarantine, it should be noted that the Earth has a comet-like tail (magneto-tail) that extends well past the Moon. The concern was that microorganisms from Earth could work their way in to the Earth's upper atmosphere, get caught in the magneto-tail and eventually get swept up by the Moon, trapping the little organisms on the Moon's surface.

501. How long does it take the Shuttle to get to orbit?

About 8 1/2 minutes.

502. For manned space missions, KSC Florida controls the launch and JSC Houston controls the mission. At what point is control transferred from the Launch Control Center (LCC) to the Mission Control Center (MCC)?

When the launch vehicle's tail rises above the top of the Fixed Service Structure (launch tower). At this time the event is announced and MCC Houston takes control.

503. What spacecraft was the first to have more than one docking port?

Skylab. It had two ports. The Multiple Docking Adapter (MDA) segment had an axial port (on the forward end) for normal operations and a radial port on the bottom side for rescue. The rescue port was never used.

504. Which manned spacecraft was the first one designed to be flown only in a vacuum?

The Lunar Module (LM) of the Apollo program.

505. What satellite system was introduced by NASA to reduce the number of ground communication and tracking stations?

Hard Suit - Soft Suit

IVA most always means work in a shirtsleeve environment and EVA means suited work outside a spacecraft in vacuum conditions. Categories that cause confusion arise when a crewmember must perform suited work inside the spacecraft. Such work may be done with the inside at a vacuum (or at a pressure too low to support life), or with the inside of the spacecraft at normal operating pressure. In the latter case, suited operations may be required because of environmental contamination.

Work done inside at low pressure (or vacuum) is usually labeled hard suit because the normal suit pressure stiffens the suit. A good example of a hard suit operation would be to patch a hole caused by a meteoroid or a piece of orbital debris, which has caused a loss of pressure in the module. Suited work inside at nominal cabin pressure is called soft suit because the pressure inside the suit can be held roughly equal to cabin pressure and still provide all life support and protection required. A soft suit operation is much easier to accomplish because the crewmember doesn't have to "fight" the suit and glove stiffness. Descriptions or procedures for suited work inside usually include options for the range of pressure differences that may be encountered.

The TDRSS (Tracking and Data Relay Satellite System) spacecraft. TDRSS (pronounced "teed'russ") uses three to four satellites in stationary orbits to relay signals from the Shuttle to ground and vice versa. Usually, only two are active with one serving as a spare. TDRSS is also used for the International Space Station. For Shuttle and the ISS communications are available for 85% of each orbit.

506. When did the Chinese first select crew candidates for space flights?

If you said, "I don't know?" you are correct. In April 2002 the media of the Peoples' Republic of China introduced over ten fighter pilots (variously reported as 12 or 14) who had been in training "for several years."

507. Which Apollo manned mission was the only one that didn't launch from the pads 39A or 39B (which were especially constructed for the Saturn V boosters)?

Apollo 7. It was assembled on, and launched from, Launch Complex 34. It was the first manned Apollo mission that used the Saturn IB. Apollo 8 through 17 used the Saturn V. The three manned Skylab missions and the Apollo-Soyuz mission also used the Saturn IB but launched from Launch Complex 39B. *See next question (Q 508).*

508. The Mobile Launcher structure was sized (height-wise) for the Saturn V Moon rocket. What modification was required to accommodate the Saturn 1B (which was 130 feet shorter)?

A four-legged platform called a "milk stool:" was added to the Mobile Launcher base to raise the spacecraft up to the level of the White Room where the crew entered the spacecraft. The "milk stool" was used for Skylab and Apollo-Soyuz missions.

509. What engineering designation did the German rocket scientists give to the rocket later called the V-2?

A-4.

510. What do the acronyms IVA and EVA mean?

IVA = Intravehicular Activity (work inside the spacecraft).
EVA = Extravehicular Activity or space-walk. *See sidebar*, **Hard Suit - Soft Suit**.

511. What major automobile company built the first stage (S-IB) of the Saturn IB rocket?

The Chrysler Corporation Space Division (CCSD).

512. Where were the Apollo spacecraft manufactured?

The Command and Service Module (CSM) was built by North American-Rockwell in Downey, California (greater Los Angeles area); the Lunar Module (LM) was built by the Grumman Aircraft Engineering Corporation (GAEC) at Bethpage, New York (Long Island).

513. What equipment aboard the Skylab was provided to repair punctures from meteoroids?

Four-inch diameter dome-shaped patches and long, tapered, carrot-shaped plugs. The domes were to be placed over holes too large for the plugs. We had no instances of meteoroid puncture.

514. What company built the IU (Instrument Unit), the brains of the Saturn boosters?

The International Business Machines Corporation (IBM).

515. Which satellite revealed the Earth to be slightly pear-shaped, with bulges in the Southern Hemisphere?

Vanguard 1, launched March 1, 1958.

516. What programming error caused Gemini 5 to land 80 miles short?

A programmer entered an incorrect value for the Earth's rotational rate. He left off two decimal places when entering the rate (360° per 24 hours instead of 360.98° per 24 hours).

517. What specialized building at the Johnson Space Center was known as the LRL?

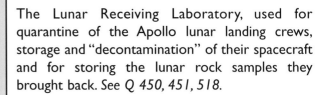

NASA Definitions

A meteoroid is a solid object larger than a molecule and smaller than an asteroid, moving through interplanetary space.

A meteorite is such an object that reaches the Earth's surface without completely vaporizing in the atmosphere.

A meteor is the light phenomenon resulting from a meteoroid's entrance into the atmosphere.

The Lunar Receiving Laboratory, used for quarantine of the Apollo lunar landing crews, storage and "decontamination" of their spacecraft and for storing the lunar rock samples they brought back. See Q 450, 451, 518.

518. How long were the astronauts kept in quarantine?

21 days. The crew quarantine was discontinued after Apollo 14. See Q 517, 450, 451.

519. What is the difference between a meteoroid and a meteorite?

A meteoroid is an object moving through space; a meteorite is a meteoroid that reaches the Earth's surface. See sidebar, **NASA Definitions**.

520. What name is given to a meteoroid that explodes when entering the Earth's atmosphere?

Bolide.

521. What European country provides launch abort landing sites for the Shuttle?

Spain. The TAL sites are at Moron and Zaragosa. In Africa Ben Guerir airport, Morocco is still maintained for use but two others have been deactivated (Dakar, Senegal and Baranjul, Gambia). See Q 51.

522. How long does it take sunlight to reach the Earth?

Eight minutes.

523. What is the name of the star closest to Earth (excluding the Sun)?

Alpha Centauri is the answer usually given (4.3 light years from Earth). If you said Proximi Centauri, give yourself a pat on the back. It is very faint, but is only 4.1 light years from us.

524. Who discovered that the planets move about the sun in an elliptical path?

Johannes Kepler, a German astronomer who lived in the seventeenth century.

525. Which Shuttle experienced a shutdown of one of its three Main Engines during launch?

Challenger (Mission 51-F, July 29, 1985, Gordon Fullerton, Commander). Because the failure occurred late in the launch they executed an Abort To Orbit (ATO) and were able to complete the mission.

526. What does the term "gravity assist" mean when applied to the path of a spacecraft?

Gravity assist is a change in velocity (speed and direction) of a spacecraft's trajectory caused by a close fly-by of a planet (where the gravity of the planet will have the greatest desired effect). The moons of a planet may also be used for this purpose. Sometimes it's called a "swing-by" or "slingshot maneuver". Voyager 1, launched in 1977, exploited this technique to cut the flight time to Neptune from 30 years down to 12 years.

527. Who was the youngest person to go into space (in the 20th century)?

Cosmonaut German Titov. He was twenty-five years old when he launched aboard Vostok 2, August 6, 1961.

528. How much does the Shuttle Launch Vehicle weigh at launch?

Four and a half million pounds.

529. How many satellites (moons) orbit the planet Mars? Extra IQ points if you can name them!

Two. They are named Phobos (fear) and Deimos (terror). Phobos and Deimos were mythical figures who drove the chariot of the Roman war god Mars. *See Q 659.*

530. How many calories are there in the daily Shuttle diet?

Approximately 3,000. This doesn't include snacks.

531. What common food preservation process is called thermostabilized by NASA?

Food sealed in cans (ordinary canned goods).

532. How much oxygen does a person need each day?

About two pounds mass. *See Figure 2,* **Daily Metabolic Balance**.

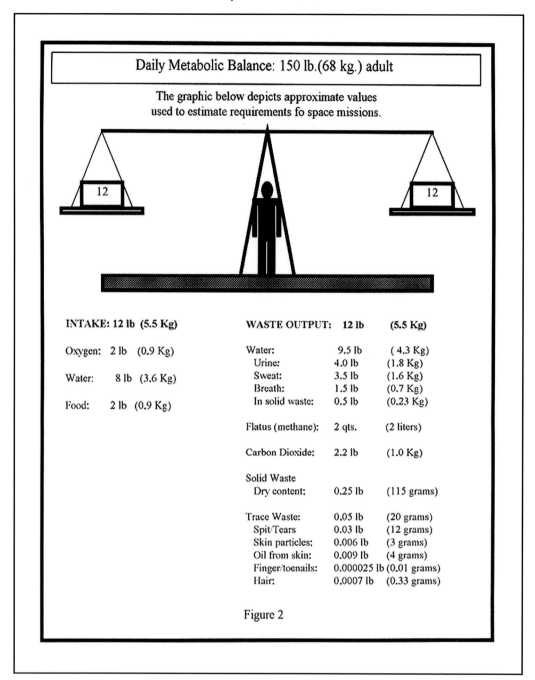

Daily Metabolic Balance: 150 lb.(68 kg.) adult

The graphic below depicts approximate values used to estimate requirements fo space missions.

INTAKE: 12 lb (5.5 Kg)

Oxygen: 2 lb (0.9 Kg)

Water: 8 lb (3.6 Kg)

Food: 2 lb (0.9 Kg)

WASTE OUTPUT: 12 lb (5.5 Kg)

Water:	9.5 lb	(4.3 Kg)
Urine:	4.0 lb	(1.8 Kg)
Sweat:	3.5 lb	(1.6 Kg)
Breath:	1.5 lb	(0.7 Kg)
In solid waste:	0.5 lb	(0.23 Kg)
Flatus (methane):	2 qts.	(2 liters)
Carbon Dioxide:	2.2 lb	(1.0 Kg)
Solid Waste Dry content:	0.25 lb	(115 grams)
Trace Waste:	0.05 lb	(20 grams)
Spit/Tears	0.03 lb	(12 grams)
Skin particles:	0.006 lb	(3 grams)
Oil from skin:	0.009 lb	(4 grams)
Finger/toenails:	0.000025 lb	(0.01 grams)
Hair:	0.0007 lb	(0.33 grams)

Figure 2

533. What does posigrade mean when used to describe a thrusting maneuver?

A posigrade thrust acts to increase the velocity of a spacecraft (that is, the thrust is in the direction it's already traveling). Retrograde is the opposite of posigrade.

534. What was the acronym for the set of instruments installed on the Moon's surface by the Apollo astronauts?

ALSEP (Apollo Lunar Surface Experiment Package).

535. How fast does the Earth move in its orbit about the sun?

18 miles per second (29 kilometers per second).

536. What is meant by redundancy when applied to spacecraft design features?

Redundancy is the duplication of components or systems to increase reliability. For critical functions the level of redundancy may be much higher than simple duplication. The Shuttle has five flight computers.

537. What material is used for the space suit helmets (Apollo to Shuttle)?

LEXAN, a polycarbonate plastic developed by the General Electric Company. *See sidebar,* **Bulletproof.**

538. Which planet's four largest moons are known as the Galilean satellites?

Jupiter. The satellites were named for 17th century Italian astronomer and physicist Galileo Galilei who discovered them using the recently developed telescope. Their specific names are: Io, Europa, Ganymede and Calisto.

539. How many sunrises can be seen by an astronaut in one Earth day (Low Earth Orbit)?

Sixteen. (Also 16 sunsets).

540. Which Apollo mission brought back the largest rock from the Moon?

Apollo 16. It was just less than 25 pounds (11.34 kilograms) when weighed on Earth.

Bulletproof

When the one-piece "bubble" helmet was introduced (during Apollo) there were a few raised eyebrows and questions arose about the helmet's survivability following hard impacts. To increase confidence in the strength of LEXAN the suit manufacturer provided a show and tell demonstrator for astronauts. It included a circular disk of the LEXAN along with a small sledgehammer and a wooden base. The base had a circular plug cut out so the plastic disc could be centered over the hole to increase the damage from hammer strikes. It was a very convincing demonstration. No one ever came close to breaking it and the demonstrator proved its worth. After I tried it once I never had a lingering doubt about the helmet strength.

541. What attachment provision held the Skylab stainless steel tableware onto the food trays?

Magnets (imbedded in the food tray).

542. Which planet has the largest moon in the solar system?

Jupiter. Its moon Ganymede is 3,280 miles (5,276 Km) in diameter, larger than the planet Mercury. If you said Saturn you're very close. Its moon, Titan, was thought to be the largest before Voyager observations. Titan's diameter is 3,220 miles (5,150 km).

543. Which manned mission had the shortest launch window?

Gemini 11. A mere two seconds were allowed to enable rendezvous with the Agena target on the first orbit. This was done to prove that Apollo astronauts could do the same thing after launch from the Moon.

544. What aerodynamic drag devices are available for use during the Shuttles approach to landing?

A body flap and speed brake (split rudder). The drag chute is deployed after landing. If you're a purist and included the aerodynamic drag of the Shuttle airframe itself give yourself a pat on the back.

545. What atmospheric light phenomena are created by particles trapped in the Earth's magnetic field?

The northern lights and southern lights. Aurora borealis (northern) and aurora australis (southern).

546. In what year did Captain Chuck Yeager break the sound barrier?

1947. The date was October 14 and the aircraft was the Bell X-1 rocket powered research aircraft. *See Q 654.*

Crazy Quote: *In discussing the future performance of aircraft: "Another popular fallacy is to expect enormous speed to be obtained. ... it is clear that ... there is no hope of competing for racing speed with either our locomotives or our automobiles." William H. Pickering, Aeronautics, June 1908.*

547. What was the propellant consumption rate of the Saturn 5 Moon rocket at liftoff?

Three tons per second (first stage).

548. The first manned Mercury mission was designated M-R3. What does M-R stand for?

Mercury-Redstone (Mercury spacecraft; Redstone booster rocket).

549. The Mercury space suit was developed from what existing military flying suit?

The U.S. Navy Mark IV Pressure Suit used for high altitude aircraft flights.

550. Which test pilot made the most flights in the X-15?

USAF test pilot Robert A. (Bob) Rushworth (34 flights).

551. Why did our first attempt to send a spacecraft to Venus go off course?

Programmers left out a character from guidance equations for the Mariner 1 launch vehicle.

552. What device is used to soften the landing as Russian spacecraft approach the Earth's surface?

Braking rockets. They're fired when the spacecraft is about ten feet (three meters) above the ground.

553. What laboratory designed the evaluation tests for the first astronaut selection?

The Lovelace Clinic in Albuquerque, New Mexico.

Neat Quote: *The testing by the Lovelace Clinic was so lengthy and invasive that the process prompted a lot of unflattering comments by the astronauts. The following is typical:* "… *it was a case of sick doctors working on well patients.*" *Wally Schirra, Mercury 7, Gemini 6, Apollo 7.*

554. Why was Deke Slayton denied the opportunity to make his scheduled Mercury flight?

A heart irregularity (idiopathic atrial fibrillation) was discovered during test runs in a centrifuge.

555. Who made the first airplane flight solely by reference to instruments, including takeoff and landing?

James H. (Jimmy) Doolittle (September 24, 1929).

556. Who was chiefly responsible for the design of the Mercury spacecraft?

Max Faget. Max was also influential in the design of Gemini, Apollo and Shuttle spacecraft.

557. Which spacecraft was the first to provide a boom used by astronauts to transfer equipment on space walks?

Skylab. A 30-foot extendible ribbon boom was used to transfer and retrieve film magazines used by solar telescopes. It was called a Film Transfer Boom (FTB) and, as a backup, a continuous loop strap (threaded through hooks at both ends [work stations]) was available to do the same thing. It was dubbed the Brooklyn Clothesline and worked quite well.

558. Which Science Pilot/Mission Specialist flew on Skylab and Spacelab?

Owen Garriott. Owen flew on Skylab 3 (second visit) and STS-9/Spacelab 1.

559. What peculiar luminous specks did John Glenn see outside his Mercury spacecraft and what did he call them?

White particles floating around the spacecraft which he called, "fireflies".

560. What part of the International Space Station is provided by Canada?

The Mobile Servicing System (MSS), a mobile platform including the Space Station Remote Manipulator System (SSRMS) or robotic arm and the Special Purpose Dextrous Manipulator (SPDM) - See Q 702. The MSS can move along the space station truss to different work positions. The SSRMS can inchworm itself across several locations.

561. How long did it take Apollo astronauts to orbit the Moon?

Two hours. Orbital velocity was just under 3600 m.p.h. (one mile per second/1.6 kilometers per second).

Canada's robotic arm aboard the STS-2.

562. What were the 16-g limit lines for Saturn launches?

Lines on a plot of altitude vs. velocity. If violated, the crew was required to initiate an abort. See sidebar, **Not Too High - Not Too Low.**

563. What was the name of the Greek philosopher credited with being the first to predict a solar eclipse?

Thales of Miletus, in 585 BC. Incidentally, as a matter of historical trivia, the eclipse was so dramatic in the Mid-east that it put an end to a war being waged between the Lydians and the Medes.

564. What type of craft did the Bell Aerospace Company propose in 1966 as a contingency method of returning astronauts from the Moon to the command ship in lunar orbit?

A single-person rocket that the astronauts could strap on and fly to orbit. It was called LEAP (Lunar Escape Astronaut Pogo). It was never developed.

565. Among the 29 Apollo astronauts, what recessive genetic traits occurred at much greater proportion than within the general American population? Name one.

Blue eyes (16 or 55%; norm = 35%), and left-handedness (7 or 25%; norm = 11%).

566. How many seconds of fuel did Neil Armstrong and Buzz Aldrin have left when they touched down on the Moon?

You're right if you said anything between 15 and 45 seconds. The numbers vary. Official and unofficial sources state variously, "less than 45 seconds", "less than 30 seconds" and some sources quote "less than 15 seconds".

567. What contaminant was transferred from the Moon to the Apollo spacecraft?

Dust from the lunar soil. The suits became quite dirty after walking around in the fine dust.

568. Why did the Apollo-Soyuz Docking Module have to include an airlock?

The air pressure in the two spacecraft was different. For docking, Soyuz was maintained at about 9½ p.s.i. (pounds per square inch) and Apollo at 5 p.s.i.. In fact, the Soyuz normally operated at just under 15 p.s.i. (Earth sea level pressure), but the cosmonauts lowered their pressure before docking to simplify the procedures for crew transfer through the docking module.

Not Too High - Not Too Low

If the booster path crossed the upper limit line called a lofting trajectory limit or the bottom limit line called a depressed trajectory limit, a subsequent abort would subject the crew to reentry forces of more than 16 g's, considered to be the maximum safe physiological limit for the crew. If the launch path appeared to be ready to cross either line, the Commander could initiate an abort which would shut down the booster rocket engines and command separation of the spacecraft from the booster thus allowing the crew to execute the appropriate launch abort mode.

569. What dictates the maximum size of Shuttle payloads delivered to the International Space Station?

The Shuttle Payload Bay dimensions (15' diameter & 60' long, roughly cylindrical limits).

InfoNote: A Transhab module proposed for the ISS would be an inflatable structure sized to fit in the Shuttle payload bay but enlarge to 26½ feet in diameter and 27½ in height after being attached to ISS and inflated. The Transhab would provide living quarters, dining accommodations and other facilities for crewmembers. As of early 2003 it had not been approved.

570. Which spacecraft was the first to maneuver from one orbit to another? Exclude reentry retrofire.

Gemini 3 (Grissom and Young).

571. Who was the first U.S. Astronaut to perform a space-walk in a Russian space suit?

Jerry Linenger, from the Mir space station with cosmonaut Vladimir Tsibliyev, using the Russian Orlan-M suit. Jerry was the first American to undock from a space station aboard two different spacecraft (U. S. Shuttle and Russian Soyuz).

572. Why are the nozzles of most liquid-fueled rocket engines surrounded by a jacket of welded tubes?

The liquid propellant is pumped through the tubes before entering the combustion chamber. Called regenerative cooling, this technique keeps the nozzle cool and warms the propellants for better combustion. The Main engines on the Shuttle use liquid hydrogen (fuel) and liquid oxygen (oxidizer); both of these propellants are classified as cryogenic (very cold). See Q 606.

573. How were stages of the Saturn V rocket transported from California to Florida?

By barges. South across the Pacific, through the Panama Canal, across the Gulf of Mexico to the Atlantic and then to the Kennedy Space Center (KSC). Some were shipped straight across the Gulf to Mississippi, for storage and later delivery to KSC.

574. The boundary that separates the sunlit and dark regions of a planet or moon is called what?

The Terminator.

575. How much jet aircraft flying time is required to apply for a pilot astronaut selection?

The Space Shuttle Endeavour, atop NASA's Shuttle Carrier Aircraft, flying over Ellington Field. (above) See Q 126.
The Space Shuttle Discovery rolls out to Launch Pad 39B at Kennedy Space Center, Florida. (bottom left) See Q 125.
A technician works to repair damage to the Space Shuttle Discovery's external tank caused by woodpeckers. (bottom right) See Q 158.

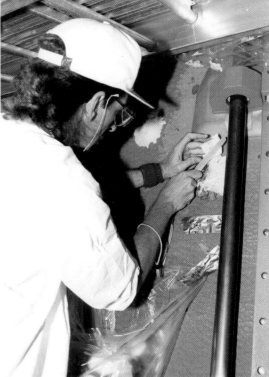

Astronaut James B. Irwin gives a military salute beside the United States flag during the Apollo 15 lunar surface Extravehicular Activity (EVA). (above) *See Q 182.*

Using the Canadarm2, the S0 (S-Zero) Truss is moved from the Space Shuttle Atlantis' cargo bay. (below) *See Q 213.*

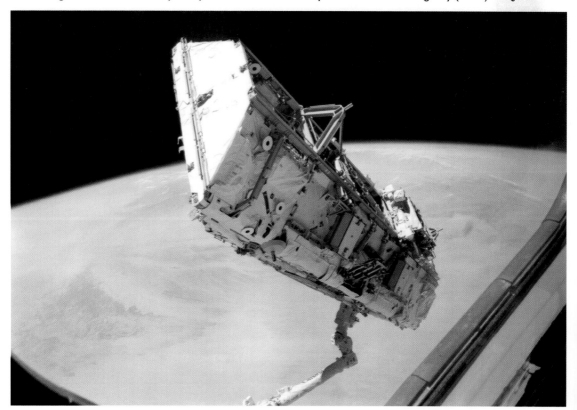

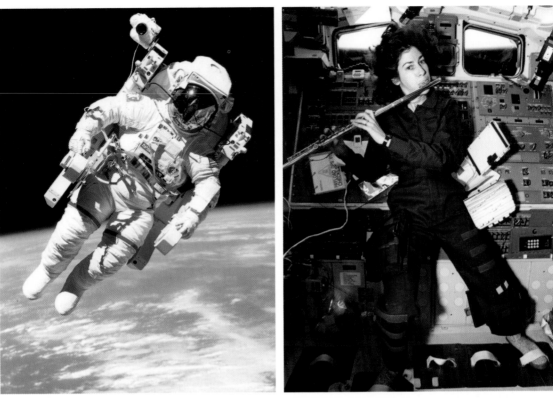

Astronaut Bruce McCandless II is the first to test the Manned Maneuvering Unit (MMU). (top left) *See Q 209.*
Astronaut Ellen Ochoa, plays a 15-minute set of flute offerings on the Space Shuttle Discovery's aft flight deck. (top right) *See Q 290.*
The KC-135 aircraft (Vomit Comet) is used to create brief periods (25-30 seconds) of zero gravity. (below) *See Q 250.*

This photo shows the "javelin" and golf ball used by astronaut Alan B. Shepard Jr., during the Apollo 14 mission. Just to the left of center lies the "javelin", with the golf ball just below it. (above) *See Q 151.*
The Super Guppy transport aircraft. (below) *See Q 259.*

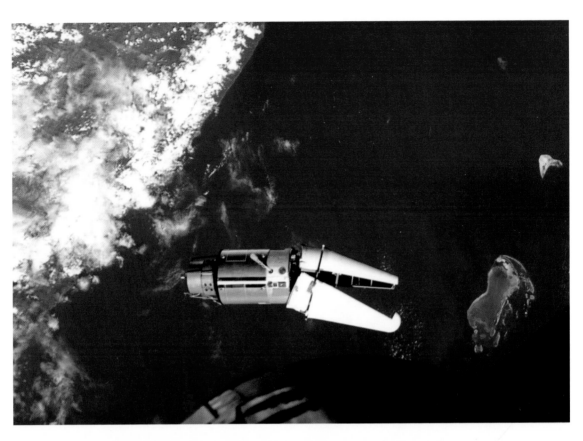

The Agena docking target for Gemini 9. Also know as the angry alligator. (above) *See Q 316.*
A photo of the Apollo Range Instrumentation Aircraft (ARIA). (below) *See Q 483.*

This view of the Earth was seen by the Apollo 17 crew as they travelled towards the Moon. (above) See Q 762.
This is the launch of Mercury-Atlas 9 on May 15, 1963. (bottom right) See Q 673.
The chimpanzee "Ham" was placed in a capsule for the Mercury-Redstone 2 test flight. (bottom left) See Q 283.

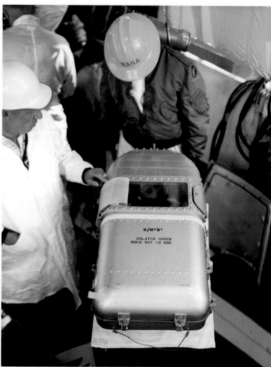

Photo of the AERCam Sprint free-flying in the vicinity of the cargo bay of the Space Shuttle Columbia. (above) *See Q 634.*
Astronaut James B. Irwin works at the Lunar Roving Vehicle (LRV) during the first Apollo 15 lunar
surface Extravehicular Activity (EVA-1). (below) *See Q 182.*

A worker monitors the giant treads of the crawler-transporter as it moves towards Launch Pad 39B. (above) *See Q 724.*
The Space Shuttle Orbiter 101 "Enterprise" separates from NASA 905, a 747 carrier aircraft. A T-38 chase plane
follows in right background. (below) *See Q 227.*

1000 hours (pilot-in-command time).

576. What was the name of the first family of Chinese rockets?

Long March.

577. Who was the first astronomer to maintain that the Earth revolves about the Sun?

The Greek astronomer, Aristarchus, third century BC. This was eighteen centuries before the 16th century Polish astronomer Copernicus revived the idea.

578. What facility in California was intended as a Shuttle launch site for polar missions?

Vandenberg Air Force Base. It was never used.

579. Which U.S. spacecraft was the first to be launched from a foreign launch center?

Uhuru, (Swahili for Freedom). It was launched from the Italian San Marco platform in the Indian Ocean east of Kenya on December 12, 1970, Kenya's Independence Day. Uhuru mapped the universe in x-ray wavelengths and discovered x-ray pulsars and evidence of black holes.

580. An electromagnetic mass driver has been proposed for launching payloads from the Moon. What problem would arise if this were tried for Earth launches?

Air friction from the Earth's atmosphere would be a problem to overcome. Vacuum conditions on the Moon make the mass driver a feasible concept for launches from the lunar surface.

581. Who made the first working model of a mass driver?

Dr. Gerard O'Neill, professor of Physics at Princeton University (1977).

582. The lowest point in the orbit of a spacecraft circling the Earth is called what?

Perigee. The highest point is called the apogee.

583. Where is the Chinese launch center for manned space missions located?

In the Gobi desert, Inner Mongolia, near the town of Jiuquan.

584. Who was the first astronaut selected from the U.S. Army?

Robert L. Stewart (Eighth astronaut selection - 1978).

585. What was the designation of the Soviet rocket intended to carry cosmonauts to the Moon?

N-1. In the West it was dubbed the G-1. From 1969 to 1972 four attempts were made to launch the huge rocket but the longest flight was 1½ minutes. All failed before the end of first stage boost.

Pitiful Prophecy: *"The successes of the Socialist state are, figuratively, a multistage rocket which will unfailingly put all peoples into the orbit of communism. A new stage of the flourishing of the Socialist system and a new stage of the general crisis of capitalism - this is the characteristic feature of our world." Pravda, March 28, 1961.*

586. What is a Whipple Bumper?

A sacrificial surface approximately 5"- 6" (12 cm – 15 cm) out from a spacecraft's primary structure that absorbs hits from meteoroids and shatters them into many smaller and less damaging particles. It's named for American astronomer, Fred L. Whipple, who proposed the concept. Note: Russian space pioneer, Konstantin Tsiolkovsky, described such a provision much earlier but his writings were not familiar to the West.

587. At what altitude above the Moon's surface did the Apollo astronauts begin their breaking maneuver for the lunar landing?

50,000 feet.

588. Which aircraft carrier recovered the Apollo 11 crew after their return from the first lunar landing?

The USS Hornet (southwest of Hawaii).

589. How long does it take the Sun to complete one revolution around our galactic center?

225 million years. Our galaxy is one of billions throughout the Universe.

590. Who performed the first docking between two manned spacecraft?

Cosmonaut Vladimir Shatalov (Soyuz 4 and Soyuz 5, January 1969).

591. What is the name of the family of rockets developed jointly by the European Space Agency and France's space agency?

Ariane.

592. From what country are the Ariane rockets launched?

French Guiana, near Kourou on the east coast of South America (The Guiana Launch Center).

593. What advantage is provided by the location of the Guiana Launch Center ?

It's located at 5° − north latitude providing near maximum benefit from the Earth's rotation. *See Q 438, 475.*

594. What causes the communications blackout (loss of radio contact) during reentry?

A blanket of ionized gas called plasma is generated by reentry heating. The plasma envelops the spacecraft and acts like a shield preventing or reducing the quality of radio transmissions. In the early 1990s NASA was able to partially correct this problem by using the Tracking and Data Relay Satellite System, exploiting a gap or region of reduced plasma that exists behind the Shuttle.

595. During reentry how long is the Shuttle in communications blackout?

The communications blackout lasts approximately 13 minutes (from about 16,700 mph at 310,000 feet to 8,300 mph at 180,000 feet altitude). By comparison the blackout period for Gemini and Apollo was just over five minutes (returning from Earth orbit).

596. What caused the first human fatality on a space mission?

Descent parachute failure. The parachute failed to deploy properly and became entangled around the spacecraft causing the death of cosmonaut Vladimir Komarov during the first flight of the Soyuz spacecraft (Soyuz 1 - April 24, 1967).

597. Who took the first photograph of a solar eclipse from space?

Buzz Aldrin, Gemini 12, November 1966.

598. Which unmanned spacecraft was the first to transmit data from the surface of another planet (Don't include the Moon.)?

Venera 7. It was a Soviet satellite that landed on Venus and lasted long enough (several minutes) to transmit environmental data from the planet's surface (December 15, 1970).

599. What is the effect on the Earth's orbit as it sweeps through the natural debris in the solar system?

It tends to make the Earth's orbit more circular or less elliptical.

More Bang For The Buck

The Ascent Stages for Apollo 11 and 12 crashed on the Moon after their orbits decayed. Starting with Apollo 14, the Ascent Stages were deliberately crashed into the Moon using pre-programmed burns of the Ascent Engine (after the crew had transferred to the Command Module, of course).

Also, starting with Apollo 14, the S-IVB Saturn stages (that provided the final boost toward the Moon – Translunar Insertion) were aimed at the Moon after the Apollo crews had extracted the Lunar Module (and gotten out of the way). The S-IVB's crashed at pre-selected spots on the Moon. These impacts were used to learn more about the Moon's internal structure using the seismic instruments left on the surface by the astronauts.

InfoNote: Assuming a homogeneous distribution of the debris in the Earth's orbital path, the "drag effect" is greater in that portion of the orbit where the Earth is moving faster. This tends to "pull in" or lower the area of the orbit at greatest distance from the Sun, making the orbit more circular.

600. What was the first U.S. satellite program dedicated to observation of the Earth's surface?

Corona, under code name Discoverer, 1960-1972. First successful launch and recovery was in August 1960.

601. What unusual technique was used to recover Discoverer return capsules?

As they descended on parachute they were snatched in mid-air by aircraft (C-119 or C-130) using a sling deployed under the aircraft. The capsules were then reeled inside the aircraft.
See Q 695.

602. The Apollo 10 Lunar Module crew returned to the Command Module in lunar orbit using the Ascent Stage. What happened to the Ascent Stage after they were through with it?

It was put into orbit around the Sun. After the crew released it the engine was fired by remote control from Earth, using all the remaining propellant. See sidebar, **More Bang For The Buck.**

603. How many items were stowed on Skylab?

Over 20,000, including 160 pounds of procedures books and reference manuals.

604. What is the difference between fuel and propellant in a liquid rocket?

Propellant usually consists of two chemicals in separate tanks, one called the <u>fuel</u> and the other called the <u>oxidizer</u>. Fuel is a propellant but a propellant isn't necessarily a fuel (It may be an oxidizer.).

However, monopropellants are sometimes used in which the propellant dissociates and expands rapidly under the influence of (a) a catalyst. eg. platinum for hydrazine, silver for hydrogen peroxide) or, (b) a change of physical conditions such as exposure to low pressure – the vacuum of space (cold gas systems). See Q 618.

605. What is the advantage of using hypergolic propellants?

No ignition source is required; they burn spontaneously when they come in contact. Also, they have a relatively long storage life onboard spacecraft when proper storage temperatures are maintained.

606. When are propellants classified as cryogenic?

Cryogenic propellants require very cold storage temperatures. e.g. Liquid hydrogen (LH_2) and liquid oxygen (LOX) are used for the Shuttle's main engines. Storage temperatures are: for LOX: below -298° F (-183° C), and, for LH_2: below -423° F (-253 ° C). See Q 572.

607. During thrusting, how is steering (direction change or control) achieved in most all rockets?

By swiveling (gimballing) the engine nozzle(s). See Q 683.

608. The point during boost when a rocket experiences the highest air loads is called what?

Max Q. Max stands for maximum; Q is the symbol for dynamic pressure or air load (Max Q = Maximum Dynamic Pressure). There is no Max Q for launches from the Moon because it has no atmosphere. For the Shuttle, Max Q is experienced just above 30,000 feet. See Q 396.

609. What kind of common garden seeds were carried on the NASA LDEF (Long Duration Exposure Facility)?

Tomato seeds. They were left in space for just under six years, and later distributed to students to plant in order to determine if they had been affected. They did grow normally, even after being in space from April 1984 to January 1990.

610. What does GPS stand for?

Global Positioning System. The GPS is a system of Department of Defense satellites used to provide accurate location of receivers on the ground. Spacecraft in orbit can also use it. Shuttle Discovery (June 10, 1998) used the GPS to update its computers' navigational

Rank Has Its Privilege

I met the Salyut 4 crew, Commander Alexei Gubarev and Scientist Georgi Gretchko at the Paris Air Show in June 1975 and they showed me through the Salyut mockup. Alexei told me a great story about reclaimed water. He pointed to the valve where they drew off the reclaimed water into a clear plastic drink bag. Then he said, "After collecting the first sample, I held it up to the light, examined it carefully, handed it to Georgi and said, 'You go first'!"

data. The International Space Station (ISS) uses GPS receivers to determine its position and attitude.

611. What was the name of the solar observatory on Skylab?

The Apollo Telescope Mount (ATM). Originally, the ATM was planned for installation in an Apollo Command and Service Module (CSM), hence the origin of the name Apollo in its designation.

612. What is the size of the International Space Station?

When fully assembled the ISS will be 356 feet wide and 290 feet long. This would extend well beyond the ends and sidelines of a regulation football field. It will have over 46,000 cubic feet of internal pressurized volume (roughly equivalent to the passenger cabin volume of two Boeing 747 jumbo jets) and a mass of just less than one million pounds.

613. What material was used as a shock absorber in the landing gear (legs) of the Lunar Module?

Crushable honeycomb material. A telescoping section in the legs allowed the legs to stroke, or compress thereby crushing the honeycomb and absorbing the shock of touchdown.

614. Which spacecraft was the first to recycle water?

The Salyut 4 Russian space station (January 1975). Water recovered from the air was recycled to potable quality. This water was condensed from water vapor in the cabin atmosphere (from exhaled air and sweat evaporation from the body). *See sidebar,* **Rank Has Its Privilege.**

615. Why did all Apollos land in the ocean?

Water landings were safer. Although designed to tolerate the impact of touch down on land, high winds could tumble the spacecraft causing a risk to the crew.

Photo of Apollo 14 preparing to splashdown in the South Pacific.

616. What animals were used as test subjects in landing impact tests for the Mercury capsule?

Pigs. Placed in contour couches (on their backs), the supine swine survived 52-g impacts, protected by a crushable aluminum honeycomb energy-absorption system. All were able to get up and walk away.

617. What term did NASA use to describe longitudinal oscillations (pumping action) in Saturn rockets?

Pogo, as in "pogo stick." A mild pogo gives the crew an impression of "chugging". A severe Pogo can cause premature engine shutdown or even destroy a rocket thus a great effort is made to minimize the amplitude or strength of the pogo oscillations.

618. What propellant was used for the attitude control rockets in the Mercury spacecraft?

Hydrogen peroxide. *See Q 604.*

619. What is the lowest spot in the world (on dry land)?

The shore of the Dead Sea in Palestine. It's 1,300 feet below sea level.

620. Why do most rockets consist of stages?

Staging enables the discard of the mass of rocket structure and propellant tanks after they are emptied during the course of launch. This reduces the amount of dead weight carried later on during launch. Russian space pioneer Tsiolkovsky originated the idea using the term "rocket-train" for a multistage rocket.

621. What odor alarmed Mike Collins when he opened the hatch to the Lunar Module after Neil Armstrong and Buzz Aldrin returned from the Moon's surface and docked with the Command Module?

An odor that smelled like burning electrical insulation. In fact, the lunar dust that permeated the air in the Lunar Module caused the smell.

622. Why is it essential for the Shuttle to open the payload bay doors shortly after reaching orbit?

To expose radiators on the inside of the doors. The radiators are needed to provide cooling for the cabin and equipment. Electronic equipment is especially vulnerable to overheating.

623. How tall was the Apollo Lunar Module?

23 feet, with landing struts extended. Overall Earth weight was 32,000 pounds, fully fueled.

624. The International Space Station will fly over what percent of the World's population?

Over 90%. Count it correct if you said anything between 85% and 95%. It will fly over 70% of the land surface of the Earth.

625. On which of the planets is its day longer than its year?

Venus. The time for one complete rotation (its day) is 243 Earth days and the time for one revolution around the Sun (its year) is 225 Earth days. See *Q 637*. Venus is also the only planet with a rotation direction from east to west (If the sun were visible from the surface it would rise in the west.).

626. Only one location of a large orbiting assembly is at true zero gravity. What is it called?

The center of mass (c.m.) of the assembly. For complex architectures, the c.m. may lie outside the physical structure of the assembly.

627. Which moon of Jupiter has currently active volcanoes?

Io (pronounced: eye' oh).

628. How many U.S. astronauts made long-term visits aboard the Russian Mir space station?

Seven. Norman Thagard, Shannon Lucid, John Blaha, Michael Foale, David Wolf and Jerry Linenger. From March 1995 to June 1998 they logged a cumulative total time of 977 days in orbit aboard Mir.

629. Astronauts aboard Discovery (STS-91, June 1998) were the first to call home using a new communications system. What was it?

A satellite telephone. It was called SHUCS (Spacehab Universal Communications System).

630. Who was the first person to fly supersonic in level flight using a standard fighter aircraft?

Robert (Bob) Hoover, chief test pilot for North American Aviation (F-100 Supersaber, 1953).

631. In the 20th century which space crew sustained the most severe reentry braking force?

Soyuz 18A cosmonauts Vasiliy Lazarev and Oleg Makarov (April 5, 1975). Following incomplete staging of the booster an abort was initiated. During reentry they experienced a braking force of over 14 g's. (Some estimates placed the g-level as high as 18 g's.)

632. How many joints are there in the Shuttle's robot arm (RMS or SRMS) ?

Three (shoulder, elbow and wrist).

633. The tail of a comet points in what direction?

Away from the Sun. After a comet rounds the Sun and moves outbound the tail precedes the comet.

634. What device(s) are used to provide ISS astronauts a view of the exterior sections of the space station not in direct view from station windows?

Video cameras, at fixed locations on external structure. On STS-87 astronauts tested a 35-pound, 14-inch diameter TV robot, remotely controlled by the astronauts from inside the space station. Called the Autonomous Extravehicular Activity Robotic Camera Sprint or AERCam Sprint, it had a 7-hour battery, a flood light and small nitrogen gas thrusters (engines) for maneuvering. Although cancelled in the late 1990s, it could be revived if the need arises.

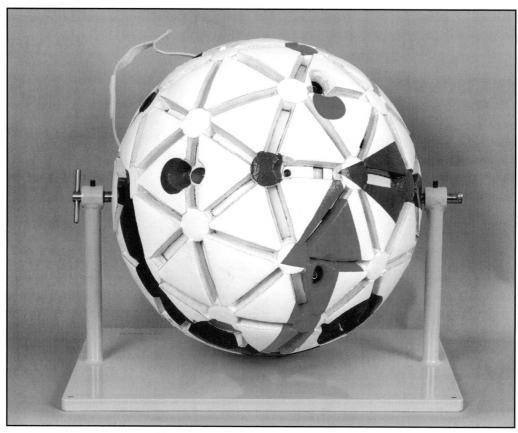

Photo of the AERCam Sprint. *See Q 634*

635. How does the Earth's magnetic field protect astronauts in low Earth orbit (less than 300 miles)?

It traps radiation from the Sun in layers or belts called the Van Allen belts. *See Q 7.* Most of the trapped radiation is above 300 miles so the shielding protects space crews below this altitude provided by the magnetic field. *See Q 477.*

636. The Shuttle's External Tank includes separate tanks for liquid oxygen and hydrogen. Which tank is larger?

The liquid hydrogen tank. It's approximately 2.75 times the volume of the oxygen tank.

637. Why are Mercury, Venus, Earth and Mars referred to as terrestrial planets?

They have solid rocky surfaces like the Earth (Terra). All other planets except Pluto are gaseous. Poor Pluto is so far away that it isn't included in the family. *See Q 625, 767.*

638. What mineral discovered on the Moon was named after the Apollo crew that brought it back?

Armalcolite, named for <u>ARM</u>strong, <u>AL</u>drin and <u>COL</u>lins (Apollo 11).

639. What is the landing speed of the Shuttle?

Approximately 225 miles per hour. The speed may be a bit higher or lower depending on Shuttle weight.

640. Why did Dave Scott (Apollo 15) drop a feather and a hammer together to the surface of the Moon?

To show that gravitational acceleration does not depend on the mass of the objects. There was no air to slow the feather in the vacuum atmosphere of the Moon.

641. What problem of space flight encountered in the 1950s was referred to as the thermal barrier?

Reentry heating. Use of a blunt shape coated with ablative material solved the problem. See Q 698.

642. What space mission was the first to return a soil sample from the Moon by remote control?

Soviet Luna 16 (September 1970). The unmanned spacecraft landed in the Sea of Fertility. A drill removed a 30 cm (foot-long) core sample of lunar soil and placed it in the return capsule, which then launched from the Moon and returned the sample to Earth.

643. What NASA term is used to describe the condition following rendezvous when two spacecraft are in close proximity and have zero relative velocity (appear motionless to each other)?

Stationkeeping.

644. What is the state vector of a spacecraft?

The state vector of a spacecraft is a mathematical expression defining two vectors: the position vector (where the spacecraft is, relative to the Earth or other body) and the velocity vector (the direction and speed it is traveling).

645. At what altitude does the Shuttle pilot lower the landing gear?

At 250 feet AGL (Above Ground Level), but give yourself credit if you answered between 200-300 feet. It takes six to eight seconds for the landing gear to extend fully.

646. At the moment of touchdown what was Neil Armstrong's heart rate (first lunar landing)?

Biomedical readouts at Houston showed it to be 156 (which just about matched the heart rate of those in the Mission Control Center). Normal pulse rate is about 70 beats per minute. Incidentally, X-15 pilots and racecar drivers have also recorded peak heart rates similar to Neil's. Tests of ordinary auto drivers' rates jump from 70 to 120 when taking the on-ramp onto a freeway. *See Q 745.*

647. Why did it take approximately three hours for the rescue team to reach Scott Carpenter after splashdown from his Mercury flight?

The Aurora 7 spacecraft overshot the intended landing point by 250 miles (May 24, 1962).

648. Who designed and built the computer used in Apollo spacecraft?

The Charles Stark Draper Laboratory at MIT (Massachusetts Institute of Technology).

649. When it ended its 18-month exploration mission why was the Lunar Prospector spacecraft programmed to crash into a crater near the south pole of the Moon (July 31, 1999)?

It was aimed to hit the bottom of a permanently shadowed crater (2½ miles deep) to see if Earth-based and space-based telescopes could detect water in the debris cloud generated by the crash. The impact produced no visible cloud. *See Q 457.*

650. What spacecraft was built to provide students a continuous view of the sunlit side of the Earth?

Triana. If successful it will remain at a fixed (relative) position between the Earth and the Sun at a distance of 935,000 miles (1.5 million kilometers). *See figure 3.* In addition to its use as an educational tool it will provide scientific data useful for studying the atmosphere and surface of the Earth (ozone and aerosol distribution, changes in the land and ocean surfaces and the sun's role in climate changes of the Earth).
Triana was named for the Lookout on Christopher Columbus' ship, Santa Maria and he was the first crewman on Columbus' crew to sight land in the "New World." Currently (2003) Triana is in storage at the Goddard Space Flight Center, Maryland. In late 2002, Triana was renamed the Deep Space Climate Observatory (DSCVR) and its launch is planned to occur following assembly of the International Space Station (late 2004 or early 2005). *See Figure 3.*

651. What device has been developed by Russian scientists to alter the mood of people in space?

Eyeglasses that can be fitted with lenses of different colors. They have reported that

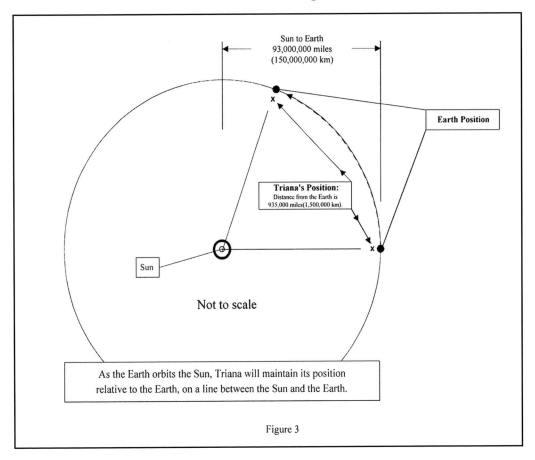

Figure 3

orange-red lenses improve concentration; yellow lenses provide a clearer view when looking at the Earth and green lenses help people relax.

652. Which instrument left on the Moon by Apollo 11 astronauts is still being used by scientists on Earth?

The Lunar Laser Ranging Experiment (LLRE). The LLRE does not require power because it merely reflects light (or radar). When zapped by a laser beam from Earth the reflector returns part of the energy, which is analyzed to measure characteristics of the Earth, the Moon and gravitational physics.

653. Convective circulation is a term used to describe the movement of liquids or gases in the vicinity of a heat source (the flame from a lighted candle, for example). Does convective circulation exist in zero-g or weightlessness?

No. On Earth the candle flame rises because it is hotter (and lighter) than the surrounding air. In the weightless environment of space it is hotter but not lighter. In still air in space the flame would go out after using up the oxygen near the flame.

654. The X-1 rocket powered aircraft was the first to exceed the speed of sound. *See Q 546.* What object was used as a model for the shape of the X-1's body or fuselage?

The .50 caliber machine gun shell (bullet). It was known to be stable at supersonic speed.

655. What is the name of the rating scale devised to indicate the likelihood of a comet or asteroid hitting the Earth?

The Torino Impact Hazard Scale. It runs from zero to ten. An object with a value of 0 or 1 has very little probability of hitting us. If an object is given a rating of ten, it's Chicken Little time! Don't even bother to get your affairs in order. Just relax and enjoy the doomsday fireworks.

656. What is the designation given to an object in our solar system whose path intersects the Earth's orbit?

It's called a Near Earth Object (NEO). *See Table 3*, **Doomsday Estimates**

Hypothetical Doomsday Estimates	
Effects of Earth collisions by NEOs (Near Earth Objects) of various sizes*	
NEO Size:	Effect
1 km dia (just over ½ mi dia)	¼ of Earth's human population killed
250 m (275' dia - a bit larger than a football field)	16 X 16 sq km (7 X 7 sq mi) obliterated
100 meters dia (at sea 1,000 km [620 mi] from shore)	30 m [100'] tidal wave @ 160 km/hr (100 mph)

In 1990 the U. S. Congress directed NASA to initiate studies and approaches to catalogue NEOs. The effort has been named the Safeguard program The goal (refined in 1998) is to catalogue 90% of near Earth asteroids with diameters of one kilometer or greater. Comets also pose a threat but are much rarer.

In January 2000 a meteor, about the size of a motorized home, entered the Earth's atmosphere over North-western Canada and exploded 15 miles (25 km) above the Earth's surface. The explosive force of the explosion was estimated to be two to three thousand tons of TNT. If such an event were to occur over a large city or military target it could be misinterpreted to be an attack. As of 2003, 600 NEOs have been identified.

* Tagliaferi, Edward, et al. *Comet and Asteroid Threat*, Space News, July 1, 2002.

Table 3

657. What defect caused the entire Space Shuttle fleet to be grounded in 1999?

An electrical short-circuit on Columbia (STS-93, July 1999). This discovery caused concern that wiring in the other Shuttles may be defective. A comprehensive inspection program was begun to discover if any problems existed in the wiring of the other Shuttles. During this process, NASA installed protective devices for wiring to prevent damage in the future.

658. In addition to wind damage, what other threat does a hurricane pose to the Kennedy Space Center facilities?

Flooding and water damage. A 15-foot (4.5 meter) flood surge, or rise above normal sea level, would cause widespread damage to facilities and space hardware being prepared for flight.

659. What fiction writer made a reference to the two moons of Mars well before they were discovered by astronomical observation?

Jonathan Swift (1667–1745). He described their approximate orbits and was surprisingly close. *See sidebar,* **How'd He Do That?**

660. In what year did President Kennedy announce the decision to send astronauts to the Moon?

1961. (May 25, 20 days after Alan Shepard's sub-orbital Mercury flight.)

661. What is the length of the Shuttle's robotic arm or Remote Manipulator System (RMS)?

50 feet.

662. What unusual ice structures were discovered when the Canadian RADARSAT mapped the entire continent of Antarctica (early 1997)?

Ice Streams.

InfoNote: Ice Streams are vast rivers of ice that flow up to 100 times faster than the ice sheet they channel through or flow through, approximately

How'd He Do That?

Irish satirist Jonathan Swift, in "Gulliver's Travels", circa 1726, refers to results of observations of the two moons of Mars by the Laputans whom Gulliver met during his travels. They are described thus:

"Where of the innermost is distant from the planet exactly three of its diameters, and the outermost five; the former revolves in the space of ten hours, and the latter in twenty-one and a half".

Actually, the innermost, Phobos, is at 1.4 diameters (5,800 miles from planet center) with an orbit of approximately 7.6 hours; the outermost, Deimos, orbits at 3.5 diameters (14,600 miles from planet center) with an orbit of 30.3 hours.

Swift was aware of a letter from the astronomer Johannes Kepler to Galileo Galilei (circa 1610) following Galileo's discovery of the Jupiter's four largest moons. Kepler suggested that, since the Earth has one moon and Jupiter has four, then it seems that Mars should have two (Mars orbits between the Earth and Jupiter.). It was a century and a half later (1877) before Asaph Hall (of the U.S. Naval Observatory) discovered them using telescopic observations and he gave them their official names. *See Q 529.*

one kilometer per year. Studies of these ice streams have produced estimates that one ice stream can deliver almost 80 cubic kilometers (17 cubic miles) of ice to the sea every year, that's enough to bury Manhattan Island with a layer of ice 1,800 meters (over a mile) deep each year. *See Q 667.*

663. Launch or rocket stage failures account for most space mission failures. What is the second most common cause for the loss of a space mission?

Software coding errors ("built-in" computer programming goofs plus command errors issued from ground control centers). Software errors may cause outright spacecraft destruction or may result in an inability to fulfill the mission (such as causing an errant trajectory or flight path from which recovery is impossible).

664. Why did Project Mercury engineers decide against jettisoning the heat shield during spacecraft descent?

During jettison tests while the capsule was dropping, the hea   shield waffled about after release and slammed back into the descending Mercury capsule.

665. What organization has developed a scale for rating solar storm intensity (similar to category ratings for hurricanes)?

The National Oceanic and Atmospheric Administration (NOAA). The Solar Storm scale ranges from S-1 (minor effects) to S-5 (extreme radiation exposure risks to space-walking astronauts, satellite electronics and Earth communications).

666. Who were the first astronauts launched by a Saturn V?

The Apollo 8 astronauts: Borman, Lovell and Anders.

667. What iceberg was so large it was given a special name and declared a hazard to shipping?

Super iceberg B10A. These huge masses of ice have also been called ice islands. *See Q 662.*

InfoNote: B10A broke off the Twaites Ice Tongue of Antarctica in 1992 and was still floating around off the south coast of Argentina into the year 2000. It was freshwater ice, almost 50 miles long, 25 miles wide and a quarter of a mile thick. During its gradual disintegration B10A spawned thousands of smaller icebergs up to a half-mile wide that broke off its edges. These "smaller" icebergs posed the greatest hazard to shipping.

668. Who was the first astronaut to test the Apollo lunar surface spacesuit on a spaceflight?

Rusty Schweickart (Apollo 9, March 1969). This test was conducted in Earth orbit, and, for the first time, a space-suited astronaut performed a spacewalk without dependence on the spacecraft for oxygen and cooling (through an attached hose or umbilical).

669. During what mission did the U.S. perform the first materials processing experiments?

Apollo 14, February 1971. Stu Roosa, Command Module Pilot, performed the experiments.

670. One scientist speculated that the Moon was covered with a thick coating of fluffy dust. What danger to landing spacecraft and crews did he think this dust would pose?

He theorized that the dust would act like "quicksand" and suck the spacecraft and astronauts into a lunar grave. This was before unmanned Surveyor satellites landed on the Moon and proved the dust theory invalid.

Crazy Quotes: " ... observ...ory research has proved that a layer of dust up to 6,000 feet thick covers the moon ... is as fine as face powder ... and is so loosely packed that no traveler would be able to walk on it." Thomas Gold, director, Greenwich Observatory. January 5, 1956.

" ... conceivably the moon has large areas where dust has accumulated to a depth as great as three thousand feet." Thomas Gold, professor of astronomy of the Harvard College Observatory, 1958.

"It isn't what people don't know that causes problems, it's what they know for sure that ain't so." Will Rogers, Humorist 1925.

671. Which crew broadcast the first live color TV from space?

Apollo 10. Astronauts Stafford, Cernan and Young, May 1969.

672. Which Apollo crew launched the first "subsatellite" into lunar orbit to study the Moon?

Apollo 15. Astronauts Scott, Worden and Irwin, August 1971.

673. Which rocket booster for manned space missions was called the "steel balloon"?

The Atlas, used for the orbital Mercury missions. To reduce weight, the booster had a paper thin, internally pressurized stainless steel skin to provide structural stiffness. See sidebar, **Boiinng**!

674. What techniques were used to study the effects of supersonic flight before supersonic wind tunnels became available (circa 1955)?

Remotely-controlled Instrumented models were dropped from high-flying aircraft and accelerated by solid rockets to achieve supersonic flight.

(((((<u>Boiiinng !</u>)))))

Originally developed as an Intercontinental Ballistic Missile (ICBM) in the 1950s, the Atlas achieved its excellent performance by reducing structural weight to an absolute minimum, employing the pressurized propellant tanks as part of the rocket's primary structure and skin. The empty weight of the Atlas was less than 2% of the propellant weight. Internal pressure was maintained between 25 to 65 p.s.i. (pounds per square inch), and, if the pressurization failed in an Atlas with full tanks, it would collapse from its own weight. The skin was only 1/100" thick!

When the Atlas was proposed as a booster for the orbital Mercury missions, Dr. Wernher von Braun was appalled, referred to the Atlas as a *"contraption"* and implied that it was too flimsy for manned flight. He was quoted as saying the astronaut *"should get a medal just for sitting on top of it before it takes off!"* To counter von Braun's criticism the Atlas designer, Karel J. Bossart of the Convair Corporation, pressurized an empty Atlas and dared one of von Braun's engineers to knock a hole in it with a sledge hammer.

When the engineer delivered a hefty blow to the side of the Atlas, the hammer bounced off, leaving the booster undamaged, but the engineer nearly got clubbed by the hammer's ricochet. He almost got a "boiiinng" in the "chops!" Following this demonstration, objections to the Atlas dissolved and it delivered flawless performance for Mercury. Atlas derivatives are still being used for satellite launches.

The Mercury-Atlas 7. See Q 673.

675. What was the thrust of the rocket engine that powered the X-15?

57,000 pounds. The Reaction Motors XLR-99.

InfoNote: Early flights were powered by two Reaction Motors XLR-11 rockets, each producing 6,000 pounds thrust (later increased to 8,000 pounds each).

676. How many patents was Dr. Goddard awarded during his rocket research?

Two hundred fourteen.

Pitiful Prophecy: *"Everything that can be invented has been invented." Charles H. Duell, Commissioner, U. S. Office of Patents, 1899.*

InfoNote: Until 1926 the German Patent Office had the same classification for airplanes as for children's toys, popular amusements and shooting galleries.

677. How many X-15s were built?

Three. One was destroyed in a crash; one is at the Air Force Museum near Dayton, Ohio and the third is on display at the Smithsonian Air and Space Museum in Washington, D. C.

678. At what University was Dr. Robert H. Goddard professor of physics?

Clark University, Worcester, Massachusetts.

679. How does the size of the Moon compare to the Sun when viewed from the Earth's surface?

They appear about the same size; both are about ½ degree across. This lucky coincidence has permitted astronomers to study the Sun's outer wispy atmosphere (the corona) during times when the Moon eclipses the Sun (passes directly in front of the Sun) blotting the sunlight and permitting the faint light of the corona structure to be observed and photographed.

680. How many German V-2 rockets were fired at allied targets during WWII?

3,745.

681. What was unique about the X-15 landing gear?

It had a conventional dual wheel nose gear but the main (touchdown) landing gear consisted of a pair of skids that extended from the aft fuselage. The X-15 landed on the dry lakebed runways at Edwards AFB, California. *See Q 697.*

682. What alternate designations were used for the Atlas booster during its early development?

HIROC and MX-774.

683. What steering technique, patented by Dr. Goddard, was used to control the Atlas flight path?

Engine nozzle gimballing (swiveling). *See Q 607.*

684. Who were the first pilots to experiment with generating brief periods of zero-gravity in aircraft?

Test pilots Chuck Yeager (USAF) and Scott Crossfield (NACA), flying jet aircraft, were able to generate about 20 seconds of weightlessness (summer and fall of 1951).

685. What item of personal equipment, intended to aid astronaut mobility in space, was one of the first devices evaluated in zero-g aircraft (circa 1958-59)?

Shoes with magnetic soles. Test subjects tried walking along the ceiling of the aircraft during the zero-g maneuvers. They weren't very effective.

686. What was the name given to the first Chinese manned spacecraft design?

Shenzhou, meaning Heavenly Ship (roughly translated). The name was suggested by Chinese President Jiang Zemin and the launch vehicle is called the Long March 2F, which has the lifting capacity comparable to the Saturn IB.

687. What name did the Chinese select for their astronauts?

Taikonauts or Yuhangyuans. I've seen both in press reports but Taikonaut appears to be preferable.

The Duties of an Astronaut

"Although the entire satellite operation will be possible, in the early phases, without the presence of man, the astronaut will play an important role during the flight. He will contribute by monitoring the cabin environment, and by making necessary adjustments. He will have continuous displays of his position and attitude and other instrument readings, and will have the capability of operating reaction controls, and of initiating the descent from orbit. He will contribute to the operation of the communication system. In addition, the astronaut will make research observations that cannot be made by instruments; these include physiological, astronomical, and meteorological observations."

NASA Project A, announcement No. 1, December 22, 1958.

688. Black mice exposed to cosmic rays in high altitude balloon flights later exhibited what change in their appearance?

A "striking increase" in the number of gray hairs in their coats.

689. Who was the first person to see the Sun rise in the west?

David Simons, during a record-setting balloon ascent to 101,000 feet (August 1957). During Simons' ascent he saw the Sun set and then, as the balloon gained altitude, he saw it rise again a bit later.

690. What special metal was used in the structure and skin of the X-15 rocket research aircraft?

An alloy of chrome and nickel called INCONEL-X. This metal could tolerate heating up to 1200° F (650° C) without loss of strength.

691. Who was the first U.S. President to attend the launch of a manned spacecraft?

Richard M. Nixon. He viewed the launch of Apollo 12, November 14, 1969.

692. For the first astronaut selection (1959) what starting annual salary range was announced?

"$8,330.00 to $12,700.00, depending upon qualifications." Insofar as what was expected of astronauts, *see sidebar,* **The Duties of an Astronaut**.

693. What derogatory expression was coined for the astronauts who would fly the Mercury capsule?

"Spam in a can" (because most space flight functions were planned to be automatic earlier in

the Mercury Program). As it turned out, the astronauts became indispensable in correcting for systems failures in the Mercury spacecraft. As noted earlier (*Q 297 and sidebar*), there was great skepticism among Soviet physiologists regarding the ability of men to function in space and a general distrust of their judgment. Some highly respected Americans also went on record in belittling the role of the astronauts.

Crazy Quotes: *"All we need to louse things up completely is a skilled space pilot with his hands itching for the controls."* John R. Pierce, research chief, Bell Telephone Laboratories, 1960.

"Putting man in space is a stunt. The man can do no more than an instrument, in fact, can do a lot less." Dr. Vannevar Bush, Chairman, Board of Governors, Massachusetts Institute of Technology, 1960.

694. What was the first man-made object to attain escape velocity from the Earth?

The Soviet Lunik I or Mechta (Russian for "dream"). Lunik I was fired toward an impact with the Moon but missed. Instead, it became the first man-made artifact to orbit the Sun. January 2, 1959.

695. What was the first satellite placed into polar orbit?

Discoverer I, early 1959. *See Q 600, 601.*

696. When were the Project Mercury personnel (referred to as the Space Task Group) transferred from Virginia to Texas?

November 1961. They organized the Manned Spacecraft Center (MSC), Houston, Texas.

697. What part of the X-15 was jettisoned (dropped off) during approach to landing?

The lower section of the ventral fin (lower tail). It was required for hypersonic stability but extended below the skids of the main landing gear; thus it had to be dropped before landing. For later flights of the X-15 the lower ventral was removed before flight for greater stability in steer climbs for altitude records. *See Q 681.*

698. Who developed and tested the "blunt body" shape that enabled vehicles to survive reentry heating?

H. Julian (Harvey) Allen of the NACA Ames Research Center, California. The research was done in 1952-53 but was not released (declassified) until years later. For his blunt body development Allen was awarded the NACA Distinguished Service Medal in 1957. *See Q 641.*

699. Which manned Mercury spacecraft did not have an observation window?

Freedom 7, Al Shepard's spacecraft. It did have an extendable periscope.

700. Who built the first white room to provide superior cleanliness for the manufacture of parts for the Mercury environmental control system?

AiResearch, for Mercury spacecraft fabrication, summer 1959. These rooms are now called clean rooms. Note: This is not the same as the White Room at the launch pad (which, incidentally, also meets "clean room" standards). *See Q 37, Q 83 sidebar and Q 202.*

701. Why were Mercury astronauts subjected to high temperature testing in heat chambers (ovens)?

Engineers were concerned that spacecraft temperatures may rise as high as 160° F for up to 20 minutes during and after reentry. They wanted to document the astronauts' ability to tolerate heat extremes.

702. What device, developed to aid in maintenance of the International Space Station, is called the SPDM?

SPDM stands for Special Purpose Dextrous Manipulator, a two-armed robot. When attached to the Space Station RMS (SSRMS), it can be positioned by the SSRMS and remotely controlled by astronauts inside the Space Station to perform maintenance tasks outside the ISS. (The acronym, SPDM, is pronounced spid'um). *See Q 560.*

703. What was the memory capacity of the computer used in Apollo spacecraft?

37K (37 kilobytes). The computer weighed about 70 pounds and required 70 watts of power. A typical personal computer with only a one-gigabit hard drive has thirty thousand times as much memory.

Pitiful Prophecies: *"I think there is a world market for about five computers."* Thomas Watson, *chairman of IBM, 1943.*

"There is no reason for any individual to have a computer in their home." Ken Olson, President *of Digital Equipment Corporation, 1977.*

704. What is the difference between docking and berthing?

In a docking operation, one module is an active vehicle and one is passive (the target). e.g. The Shuttle docks with the International Space Station (ISS). During the ISS assembly phase, after docking to the ISS, the Shuttle or Station RMS may remove a module from the Shuttle payload bay, maneuver it to its assembly location on the ISS and position it for motorized attachment. This operation is called berthing. The motorized attachment that brings the two parts firmly together executes the mating.

705. What is the volume of bulk trash produced each day by a Shuttle astronaut?

Approximately a half cubic foot (864 cubic inches). That's the volume of a box one-foot square and six inches deep. Shuttle crewmembers use a compactor to reduce the volume to 20% of the original volume before storing the trash.

706. The dogs used by Russians as test subjects for rocket and space flights had what in common?

They were all female. It was simpler to design urine collection equipment for female dogs.

707. What unusual procedure was required when preparing Skylab canned food?

They were "canned' in a special low pressure facility. These items were contained in soft aluminum "flip-top" cans, and then stacked in sturdy "over cans" which held ten of the smaller cans. Skylab cabin pressure was five pounds per square inch (5 psi.), one-third of Earth's pressure at sea level (14.7 psi.). If the items had been canned at normal atmospheric pressure, the soft aluminum cans would have swelled up or exploded when exposed to the low pressure of Skylab.

708. The shortest air travel distance between two points on Earth lies along a path called what?

A great circle route. A string stretched between two points on an Earth globe establishes a great circle route. Lindbergh flew a great circle route on his flight from New York to Paris (1927).

709. What did the Apollo 14 crew do when the abort light lit up during descent to the Moon?

LM Pilot, Edgar D. (Ed) Mitchell gave it a tap with his penlight (flashlight) and it went out. *See sidebar,* **Solder Balls**.

710. What rocket stage served double duty and was a part of two different NASA rocket boosters?

The S-IVB. It was the third stage of the Saturn V Moon rocket and the second stage of the Saturn IB.

711. The Moon's density is what percentage of the Earth's?

60%

Solder Balls

The crew and ground technicians were fairly certain the erroneous indication was caused by solder balls. During manufacture, small components were sealed with a hot metal plate to prevent contamination from entering the part from the outside environment. Occasionally there was sufficient heat applied to melt solder from joints on the inside of the component. This created balls and slivers that floated around and some were large enough to complete an electrical circuit. After a second occurrence, Ed pulled circuit breakers to inactivate the circuit controlling the abort light and the descent to the Moon continued.

Solder balls have created problems from the days of the Mercury program all the way into the early Shuttle era. One solution for the aggravating problem was to coat the inside of the component with a sticky substance called getter, which acted like flypaper to trap and hold the maverick solder balls. It was a low-tech approach for a high-tech industry.

712. Which planet in our solar system has the most moons?

Uranus. As of August 6, 1999, two new moons of Uranus were discovered raising its total to twenty.

713. Which U.S. manned spacecraft made the first steering reentry controlled entirely by computer?

Gemini 11, September 15, 1966.

714. For spacecraft reentering the atmosphere from Earth orbit what altitude is referred to as the Entry Interface (EI)?

400,000 feet, approximately 75 miles (120 kilometers). This is the point during reentry when drag forces start to increase significantly.

715. Astronauts doing spins and tumbles in zero-g can control their rotation rate by extending/retracting their arms or by doubling up their torsos or straightening up and extending their arms above their heads. What basic law of physics are they exploiting when they exert such control?

The Conservation of Angular Momentum. After starting a spin with arms extended the rate will increase when the arms are pulled in. Ice skaters use the same technique.

716. Why would an astronaut find it difficult to do a space walk on Mars' moon, Phobos?

The surface gravity of Phobos is so weak that he would be in danger of launching himself with every step if he tried to walk. A 400-pound astronaut (Earth weight including suit) would weigh less than half a pound on Phobos.

717. What name is given to the force that tends to make long slender objects (or spacecraft) line up so that they keep pointed roughly toward the center of the Earth as they move around in orbit?

Gravity Gradient Torque (or Gravity Gradient Force). An orbiting object that achieves this alignment is said to be gravity gradient stabilized (ggs). In fact, the object merely has to have one dimension slightly greater than the others. The Moon is ggs in its orbit around the Earth because it is slightly egg-shaped with the "pointy" end facing the Earth. That is why we always see the same face or surface from Earth (near side).

718. How far apart are the Shuttle launch pads (pads 39A and 39B)?

8,700 feet (about 1.65 miles or 2.64 kilometers).

InfoNote: The separation of the pads was dictated by the size and explosive energy of a fully fueled Saturn V used in the Apollo Program. This separation assured that a worst-case explosion on one pad would not wreck the other one. Their distances from the VAB are 3.4 and 4.2 miles for 39A and 39B, respectively. Incidentally, a third pad, 39C, was considered in the early 60s but dropped from planning.

719. The device developed by The Jet Propulsion Laboratory during W.W.II to aid aircraft in takeoff was called JATO (Jet Assisted Takeoff), but actually it was a rocket. Why did the developers use the less accurate designation, "jet"?

Because "the word, 'rocket' was in such bad repute," according to CalTech scientists working on the project at that time. They had witnessed the nasty treatment accorded Dr. Goddard by fellow academicians and did not want to be demonized in the same way. Later, the term, RATO (Rocket Assisted Takeoff) was introduced but most pilots still referred to it as JATO.

A Payne in the Neck: *In a letter to Dr. Robert H. Goddard, explaining the rejection of a technical paper Dr. Goddard had submitted for publication, "… (regarding your) paper, 'On the Possibility of Navigating Interplanetary Space', … the possibility is so remote is it worthwhile to publish it? …. the impossibility of ever doing it is so certain that it is not practically useful. You have written well and clearly, but not helpfully to science as I see it. Hoping you will understand me, I return your paper with thanks." William W. Payne, Editor, Popular Astronomy, 1908.*

720. The engineering designation of the Shuttle Columbia is OV-102. What does "OV" stand for?

Orbiter Vehicle.

721. What common household cleaning product was used to coat the inside of Apollo-era helmets to prevent moisture condensation (and fogging) on the inside of the transparent helmets?

Joy® liquid detergent. During Gemini spacewalks, hard-panting astronauts experienced

Jumping for Joy

Skylab had a rather sterile sensory environment. The walls and most of the lockers were a neutral beige color and even the Neutrogena® soap and shampoo had the scent removed, rather than using "off-the-shelf" products. When we coated our helmets with the Joy we all reacted with delight. Aha! They didn't remove the lemon scent from the Joy. We really got a kick out of smelling the pleasant lemon aroma, as we got ready for space walks.

temporary reduction of visibility when their breath condensed on the inside of their helmet and fogged up their face-plates. *See sidebar,* **Jumping for Joy**.

722. The paths of spacecraft in high Earth orbit are disturbed (changed slightly) by the gravitational attraction of the Sun and the Moon. What do trajectory analysts call such disturbances?

Perturbations. *See Q 465.*

723. How many people are in the on-board crew to operate the giant crawler-transporter (CT) when it hauls the Shuttle to the launch pad?

Twenty-two.

724. What is the weight of each shoe (or track segment) in the tracks of the CT?

One ton (2,000 pounds).

725. What term does NASA use to describe the flight attitude of the International Space Station?

Torque Equilibrium Attitude (TEA). By maintaining this attitude, (gravity gradient) torques caused by the Earth's gravity on the ISS are kept in balance. As the ISS orbits the Earth the "bottom" of the ISS is always facing the Earth, thus, the ISS does one full rotation (outside loop) during each orbit.

726. Which U.S. manned spacecraft had a heat shield made of metal?

Freedom 7, Al Shepard's Mercury spacecraft. It had a heat shield made of beryllium.

727. What event created a new radiation belt above the Earth in 1962?

A repair crew works on a broken shoe on the crawler-transporter (CT). *See Q 724.*

A high atmosphere nuclear bomb test over the Pacific Ocean (by the U.S. Atomic Energy Commission). This new radiation zone was lower than the inner Van Allen belt, but weakened rapidly and did not pose a threat to orbiting astronauts.

Conventional Wisdom: *Speaking about the atomic bomb to President Truman in 1945: "That is the biggest fool thing we have ever done. The bomb will never go off, and I speak as an expert on explosives." Admiral William Leahy.*

728. What term was coined by NASA spacecraft test personnel to describe a problem that might occur in one test but not be encountered during later tests?

A glitch.

729. At what angle is the Earth's rotational axis tilted to its orbital plane around the Sun?

23½° (23° 27'). This tilt is responsible for the four seasons of the year in the temperate zone.

730. What region of the Earth experiences the least seasonal variation?

The equatorial region.

731. How do the seasons in the northern hemisphere compare to those in the southern hemisphere?

They are reversed. When it's winter in the northern hemisphere it's summer in the southern hemisphere and vice versa.

732. What company manufactures the heat-resistant tiles that protect the Shuttle during reentry?

The Johns Manville Corporation.

733. How many stars were designated as navigation stars for the Apollo navigation system?

Thirty-seven. These stars were (roughly) distributed uniformly around the celestial sphere (the heavens).

734. What did Wally Schirra do to prove that Gus Grissom had not activated the Mercury hatch jettison control after landing in the Atlantic (causing the spacecraft to sink)? See Q 153.

Wally waited until he and his Mercury spacecraft were onboard the recovery ship and then he deliberately blew the hatch by pushing the jettison plunger control. The recoil of the plunger cut through Wally's metal-reinforced glove, cutting his hand, showing that Gus couldn't have blown the hatch manually without receiving a similar injury.

735. What easily observable Earth feature can an astronaut use to tell if a storm cloud pattern below is in the northern or southern hemisphere?

The spiral pattern of a storm system. If the lower cloud system is a clockwise pattern it's in the southern hemisphere and, if counter clockwise, it's in the northern hemisphere.

736. What professional group at the Kennedy Space Center was referred to as "frogs"?

All inspectors were called frogs.

InfoNote: Because they had to be a bit hard-nosed they weren't the most popular workers and the "frogs" didn't relish their role. When one was asked what it was like to be an inspector he gave the example of two men riveting. One guy holds the rivet gun and the other guy holds a metal bar to "buck" the rivet (to flatten the rivet as the man with the rivet gun hammers away on the rivet head).
He said being an inspector was like doing the bucking while everyone else was having at him with rivet guns. Someone responded, "you mean like **rivet, rivet, rivet**." Well, that's how people imitate a frog sound, thus the title, frog, was coined. The KSC workers

weren't through. They further classified the inspectors as Pond Frogs, Tree Frogs and Horny Toads (the latter is a vernacular term in the South for horned frogs, which are actually lizards).

737. What percent of the Earth's surface is land?

Approximately 30%.

738. Who was the first Hispanic woman to fly in space?

Ellen Ochoa. She was a Mission Specialist on STS-56, April 1993. See Q 290.

739. Which astronaut was awarded the French Legion of Honor?

Colonel Eileen Collins, 6 September 2000. The Ambassador of France to the United States presented the award, commending her for fostering a cooperative relationship between France and NASA, as well as her spirit of cooperation with French astronauts.

740. What hazard stopped the construction of the perimeter fence at the Mississippi Test Facility (MTF) in 1963?

Hordes of salt marsh mosquitoes were so thick that workers walked off the job until they received protection. An entomologist from the Bureau of Public Health in Washington finally solved the problem. See sidebar, **The Sting**.

741. What extreme methods did photographers employ to photograph Neil Armstrong and his family before the Apollo 11 mission (first lunar landing)?

They climbed 30-foot-high oak trees across the back fence from Neil's swimming pool. I was aghast when I heard him report it during an astronaut group meeting with our attorney. The trees were on my property. When Neil saw my reaction he

The Sting

The MTF site was selected for its remote location and access to the Mississippi River via the Pearl River. The area was not exactly a tourist Mecca. Wild hogs with bad dispositions abounded and roamed the area. The swamps were alive with millions of snakes. These were mild problems compared to the mosquitoes. 1963 was a vintage year for the salt marsh critter and they made the national news. Numerous cattle in the area were killed by breathing in the mosquitoes. The sheer mass of mosquitoes filled their lungs and the cattle suffocated. As for the workers, an entomologist studying the problem counted up to 200 mosquitoes per minute landing on them, even when they weren't swarming. None of the commercial repellants worked for more than 10 minutes.

When the workers walked off the job, NASA appealed for help from the entomologist. He told them to buy the cheapest, smelliest perfume they could find, mix it with linseed or cottonseed oil and have the workers rub it all over their bodies. Voila! This stuff worked for up to three hours and the workers were able to finish the fence.

The MTF was used to test the giant F-1 engine (1.5 million pounds of thrust) used in the Saturn V first stage and the J-2 engine (200,000 pounds of thrust) used in the second and third stages. The MTF was renamed the Stennis Space Center in 1988, to honor Senator John Stennis of Mississippi. See Q 740.

hastened to add, "Now don't touch those trees; this will all be over in a couple of weeks."

742. How many people have flown in space?

As of 1 January 2003, 427 people had flown in space on 237 missions. This does not include seven of the eight civilian and military X-15 test pilots who flew above 50 miles altitude (Adams, Dana, Knight, McKay, Rushworth, Walker and White). Joe Walker flew the highest, just above 67 miles, more than 100 kilometers. *See Q 273.*

743. What was the name of the first rocket launched from Cape Canaveral?

Bumper 8, launched in August 1950. It was a two-stage rocket with a German-built V-2 as the first stage and a U.S. built WAC-Corporal as the second stage.

744. What attorney served as legal council for Apollo-era astronauts?

Louis (Lou) Nizer, a well-known attorney in the 1960s, provided legal advice without fee.

745. Before manned flights were accomplished, medical "experts" had predicted "dire consequences" for a person going into space. Name one of these consequences?

Inability to swallow (eat or drink); cardiac arrest (heart failure); rapid heart rates leading to unconsciousness; brain damage; difficulty in breathing during high g-forces; complete loss of bodily control [inability to urinate/defecate (also, inability to stop urinating)]; inability to sleep (inability to stay awake); delusionary behavior (going crazy); inability to think logically; loss of orientation; blindness; nausea and vomiting; sudden and undetected ulcers. This is only a partial list.

Two items in this list were actually observed: Bouts of nausea and vomiting are experienced by about half of the people who go into space but all symptoms disappear after three days. Rapid heart rates as high as 150 have been observed but did not affect performance. The heart rates are no higher than those experienced by X-15 test pilots and racecar drivers. Incidentally, average drivers exhibit heart rate spikes of 120 when pulling into freeway traffic from on-ramps. *See Q 646.*

746. Which Apollo astronaut was the oldest one to land on the Moon?

Al Shepard. He was 47 years old when he landed on the Moon.

747. Who was the first woman to serve as Pilot on a Shuttle mission to the International Space Station?

Pamela Ann Melroy, aboard Discovery, Shuttle Mission STS-92, October 2000, the Space Shuttle Program's 100th mission.

748. What group planned a demonstration to protest the launch of Apollo 11 (1st lunar landing)?

The Southern Christian Leadership Conference (SCLC).

InfoNote: The SCLC was lead by Rev. Ralph Abernathy and Hosea Williams in a "Poor People's Campaign," headed by a mule-drawn wagon. NASA Administrator, Thomas Paine, along with NASA's Public Information Officer, Julian Scheer, met Rev. Abernathy as they approached the Kennedy Space Center. Dr. Paine explained to Rev. Abernathy that he was a member of the NAACP (National Association for the Advancement of Colored People) and that he had genuine sympathy for their campaign but that stopping the launch would not aid their cause.

Paine invited a representative group of Rev. Abernathy's Conference to view the launch as official guests of NASA and, further, they would be located where they could have free access to the media to air their grievances. They accepted. A NASA bus picked up 100 SCLC members the next morning (with a box lunch on every seat). They viewed the launch without incident and made their statements to media representatives.

The Most

Eight Firsts scored by Apollo 8

1. First manned flight of the Saturn V.

2. First manned vehicle to escape the Earth's gravitational field.

3. First use of a computer with navigation and guidance capability to provide onboard autonomy.

4. First manned vehicle in lunar orbit.

5. First close-up view by humans of another celestial body.

6. First time that men were exposed to solar radiation beyond the Earth's magnetic field.

7. First vehicle to thrust out of lunar orbit.

8. First manned spacecraft to reenter the Earth's atmosphere from another celestial body.

749. What is a "rockoon"?

A rocket launched from a high-altitude balloon, enabling the rocket to achieve a higher altitude.

750. Which spacecraft splashdown was the first to be covered live by TV?

Gemini 6, December 16, 1965, astronauts Wally Schirra and Tom Stafford.

751. Which Apollo space mission racked up the largest number of "space firsts"?

Apollo 8. See *sidebar*, **The Most**.

752. What is the name of the airfield at the Kennedy Space Center where the Shuttle lands?

The Shuttle Landing Facility (SLF).

753. How many tires are there on the Shuttle landing gear?

Six. Two on each main landing gear and two on the nose gear.

754. Who was the first woman to fly solo in an aircraft?

Madam Thérèse Peltier, a French woman. She was the first woman airplane passenger, July 8, 1908 and, later that summer, she took flight instruction and made several solo flights.

755. Which Apollo mission landed the farthest from the lunar equator?

Apollo 15. Dave Scott and Jim Irwin landed their Lunar Module, Falcon, near Hadley Rille, approximately 26 degrees north of the Moon's equator. Three Apollo missions landed north of the equator (Apollos 11, 15 and 17) and three landed south (Apollos 12, 14, and 16). *See Appendix B:* **Lunar Landing Sites**.

756. What did the acronym SMEAT mean during the Skylab program?

Skylab Medical Experiment Altitude Test. SMEAT was a 56-day pre-flight ground test conducted in an altitude chamber (26 July - 20 September 1972). The crewmembers for this test were Bob Crippen, Bill Thornton and Karol (Bo) Bobko who validated procedures and equipment performance.

757. In addition to fire extinguishers what other provision for fire fighting was installed on the Skylab space station?

A 40-foot fire hose connected to the water distribution system. This wouldn't have been much good against an electrical fire but could have been used on smoldering surfaces.

758. During the Apollo program which three astronauts were nicknamed, Al? Name two.

Al Shepard, Al Bean and Al Worden.

759. What was the designation (name) of the first stage of the Saturn 5 Moon rocket?

S-1C, built by the Boeing Company.

760. What was the original name of the NASA Vehicle Assembly Building (VAB) at the Kennedy Space Center?

Vertical Assembly Building. The Air Force already had a building called the Vehicle Assembly Building but most people referred to the new NASA building as the Vehicle Assembly Building, and it stuck.

761. True or False: The VAB is so large and tall that rain clouds can form in it?

False. This fiction was very popular in the late 1960s and for a while I was a believer. This contention was based partially on fact. When the huge doors of the VAB are opened even partially, the warm, moist Florida air enters and rises to the top of the VAB. The water condenses on the ceiling and then drips down. In 1969 Ron Evans and I were at the 300-foot level supporting a test and Ron told me to hold out my hand from the railing. I did and tiny droplets of water hit in my palm. It was from condensate dripping but this did not come from rain clouds.

762. Which crew was the only one that has ever seen the Earth's South Pole from space?

The Apollo 17 crew (Cernan, Evans and Schmitt). In one of their photographs, virtually the entire continent of Antarctica is visible as a distinct snow-covered mass.

A view of Earth from Apollo 17. This photo shows Antarctica's south polar ice cap.

763. When were custom-fitted contour couches first introduced to support astronauts during high acceleration or 'g' forces?

1958, at the Langley Aeronautical Laboratory, Virginia, and first tried by Robert

Champine, a test pilot, who served as a test subject in July. Later they were custom fitted for each Mercury astronaut.

764. Which was the longest Shuttle mission of the 20th century?

STS-80. In November 1996 Space Shuttle Columbia logged just under 18 days of space flight time.

765. Which Shuttle astronaut's nickname is Pinky?

Mission Specialist, George D. Nelson.

766. Which space crew was the first to be tracked by a ground-based laser?

Skylab 4 (third manned mission). Jerry, Ed and I could see a ¼ watt orange laser from a distance of 1,000 miles. The laser was aimed at us from the Goddard Spaceflight Center, Greenbelt, Maryland.

767. Where is the Kuiper Belt located in relation to our solar system?

The Kuiper Belt is an ill-defined and roughly circular (donut) region beyond the planet Neptune.

InfoNote: The thinking is that, when disturbed by other bodies, objects could spiral in to the inner solar system and become asteroids or comets. Periodic (recurring) comets are thought to originate from this band. In June 2002 astronomers at the California Institute of Technology discovered a spherical body in the Kuiper Belt. It's half the size of Pluto and was named Quaoar, (pronounced kwa' o-ar).
Current opinion of astronomers is divided over whether Pluto should be regarded as a planet, some saying that Pluto is really a Kuiper Belt object. The discovery of Quaoar seems to add credence to the claim that Pluto is a renegade from the Kuiper Belt rather than a planet. See Q 473.

768. Which Apollo astronaut worked for a "think tank" before his selection by NASA?

Walt Cunningham, Apollo 7. Walt worked for the Rand Corporation.

769. Just after liftoff, which Astronaut Commander said, "We can fix anything!"

Pete Conrad, Skylab 2 (1st visit to Skylab). They did fix it! See Q 385.

770. What concept has been proposed to back up the records of human civilization and the natural world (similar to making a rescue disk for a computer's hard drive)?

It is called the Alliance to Rescue Civilization (ARC).

InfoNote: Recent attention to the risk posed by asteroids and comets colliding with the Earth, not to mention natural calamities such as volcanoes, earthquakes, nuclear war and computer crashes on unprecedented scale, has led some to initiate the ARC effort. The idea would be to create an archive repository and stash it on the Moon for safekeeping and future use.

The implication is that this archive would include DNA coding for Earth biota as well as the history of civilization. This effort would be a logical extension of the Safeguard program that has the mission of cataloguing 90% of the one kilometer (or greater) Near Earth Objects in our solar system. ARC is envisioned as an international cooperative undertaking. *See Q 656.*

771. Which aircraft was the first to use reaction control engines (rockets) to control attitude in flight at high altitude?

The X-1-B, late 1950s. The X-15 was the first aircraft to use reaction controls routinely during test flights.

772. Which is the only Capital City that lies on the Earth's equator?

Quito, Ecuador.

773. What is a parsec?

A parsec is a measure of distance used by astronomers. A parsec is approximately equal to 19 trillion miles (31 trillion kilometers). It is the distance from Earth at which ½ the diameter of the Earth's orbit makes an angle of one arc second. There are 3,600 arc seconds in an angle of one degree.

774. What is a light year?

A light year is the distance light travels in one year, approximately 6 trillion miles (9.5 trillion kilometers). A parsec = 3 ¼ light years (approximately).

775. Which manned spacecraft was the first to use gyroscopes for attitude control?

Skylab. The units called control moment gyroscopes (CMGs) held the Skylab steady for making observations of the Sun and were also used to maneuver Skylab for studies of the Earth. The CMGs were backed up by cold gas thrusters called the Thruster Attitude Control System (TACS).

776. Who received the first birthday card in space?

Yours truly. My daughter Layna worked with a communications technician to design it and it was transmitted to the Skylab teleprinter. Pete Conrad was the first astronaut to celebrate a birthday in space, his 43rd (June 2, 1973 aboard Skylab).

777. Who was the NASA dietician that developed the condiments for Skylab food?

Rita Rapp. *See Q 364.*

778. Who was the only Science Pilot to fly the Astronaut Maneuvering Unit in Skylab?

Owen K. Garriott.

779. What was the first religious rite performed on the Moon?

Christian Communion by Buzz Aldrin (Apollo 11).

780. Which spacecraft was the first to have a dedicated area for a crew wardroom?

Skylab.

781. Who was the first astronaut to dislocate a joint in space?

Pete Conrad on Skylab 2 (first visit). While doing some energetic acrobatics Pete trapped a finger between two lockers and dislocated a finger joint. Science Pilot Joe Kerwin, a medical doctor, fixed the problem quickly.

782. Which astronaut had the longest time between space flights?

John Glenn. (February 1962 to October 1998), 36½ years between flights.

783. Why was John Glenn's reentry more spectacular than all the other Mercury reentries?

The retrorocket package was left attached to the heat shield because a warning light indicated the heat shield was loose. While it burned off during reentry it created a fiery stream of metal fragments in addition to hot gasses from the heat shield. The warning light was an erroneous indication.

784. What flight was the first launch of a spacecraft with a crew of five on board? (six? seven? eight?)

STS-7 (1st crew of five), STS-9 (1st crew of six), Shuttle mission 41-G (1st crew of seven), Shuttle mission 61A (1st crew of eight).

785. Which X-15 pilot set the speed record for winged flight?

William J. (Pete) Knight. On 3 October 1967 he attained Mach 6.70 (4,520 m.p.h.), a record that stood until the Shuttle Columbia returned from space on 14 April 1981. See Q 495.

786. Which astronauts have airfields named after them (name one)?

Tom Stafford (Municipal airport at Weatherford, OK); Gus Grissom (Grissom AFB, IN); Bill Pogue (Municipal airport at Sand Springs, OK). The Onizuka Air Force Station, Sunnyvale, CA is named after Ellison Onizuka who died in the Challenger accident, January 28, 1986.

787. What training was given to Science Pilots from the Apollo era that was not given to Mission Specialists of the Shuttle era?

Pilot training. All members of Astronaut selections 4 and 6 were assigned to U. S. Air Force pilot training classes. Some did not graduate from flying school and left the Astronaut office. In the Shuttle era, many Mission Specialists were accomplished pilots but served in technical/scientific capacities instead of being classified as Pilot Astronauts.

788. When was the Congressional Space Medal of Honor first awarded?

October 1, 1978. Six were awarded. The recipients were: Neil Armstrong, Frank Borman, Charles (Pete) Conrad, John Glenn, Virgil I.(Gus) Grissom (posthumously), and Alan Shepard.

789. In what year was the Russian Space Station Mir deorbited?

2001. (March 23)

790. What percentage of a rocket's total weight is propellant?

90 – 95%

791. What pair of satellites made the first successful fly-by of Halley's comet?

Russian satellites, Vega 1 and Vega 2. Vega 1 on March 6, 1986 and Vega 2 on March 9.

792. Which astronauts are dubbed "Cape Crusaders"?

Those working at the Cape (Kennedy Space Center) in support of upcoming missions.

InfoNote: The name, Cape Crusader, arose early in the Shuttle program. Prior to that time support crewmembers were called Redshirts by KSC personnel. Redshirts of earlier programs were not on the prime or backup crew but were assigned to specific missions to relieve the workload on the prime and backup crews. The term, Redshirt came from the game of football. On football teams the first and second-string players use Redshirts for scrimmage opponents but Redshirts don't play in games with other teams.

793. What risk to spacecraft equipment is created by exercising astronauts?

Floating droplets of sweat. If not toweled up or absorbed by clothing the sweat droplets may drift around and contaminate equipment.

794. What caused astronaut Ed White to say, "It was the saddest moment of my life"?

Orders to terminate his space walk on Gemini 4.

795. What simple production change reduced the weight of the Shuttle's External Tank (ET)?

Omitting the painting. This reduced the ET weight by 595 pounds. The first Shuttle to be launched using an unpainted tank was STS-4, June 27, 1982.

InfoNote: Two years of redesign (1980-81) trimmed some 7,000 pounds from the tank (compared to the ET used by STS-1, April 1981). Omitting the painting was part of this weight reduction. In 1998 (with STS-91) NASA introduced a Super Lightweight External Tank (SLWT), 7,500 pounds lighter and 30% stronger than the standard ET. The weight reduction was accomplished by using an aluminum lithium alloy for the propellant tanks. Because the ET is taken almost into orbit any weight savings on an ET converts directly into payload the Shuttle can carry.

796. Which Apollo astronaut had no middle name?

Michael Collins, Apollo 11, July, 1969.

797. How are the Shuttles solid rockets recovered for reuse?

After they are jettisoned (discarded) during launch they descend by parachute into the Atlantic Ocean and are picked up by retrieval ships, Freedom Star and Liberty Star. The ships tow them back to the Kennedy Space Center where they are disassembled to start the process of refurbishment.

798. What U. S. launch attempt was dubbed "Flopnik" by the media?

The attempt to launch the Vanguard TV-3 in December 1957. It collapsed on the launch pad in a ball of fire as millions of people were watching on TV.

799. How many "astrochimps" were selected to support Mercury program tests?

Six chimpanzees were selected. They received training at Holliman Air Force Base, New Mexico and the Cape Canaveral Air Force Station, Florida.

800. What was written on the commemorative plaque left on the Moon by the Apollo 17 crew?

"Here man completed his first exploration of the Moon, December 1972 AD. May the spirit of peace in which we came be reflected in the lives of all mankind".

Final Quote: *"Man's quest cannot stop short of trying to probe the heart of the mystery of the Universe."* Arnold J. Toynbee, Historian.

Photo of the Apollo 17 plaque that was left on the Moon.

Appendix A: Naming of Spacecraft

From the Mercury Program through the Apollo lunar missions astronauts were permitted to name their spacecraft in an "off again – on again" policy. The practice of allowing crews to name their spacecraft was formally discontinued starting with the Skylab missions. Although the Shuttle spacecraft are given names they were selected by NASA officials and not by the astronauts (except for one case, in which the White House influenced the selection of the name, "Enterprise." (See Q 227). The Shuttles' names and Program names such as Mercury, Gemini, Apollo, Skylab, Apollo-Soyuz, Space Shuttle, Space Station Freedom and International Space Station (Alpha) were all decided at high level, albeit, sometimes after a NASA contest. e.g. "Skylab" and "Space Shuttle."

Sometimes the spacecraft-naming process became controversial and resulted in battles of will between the flight crews and self-appointed screening experts at NASA headquarters. Gus Grissom almost ran afoul of the approval loop but won out in the end. See sidebar, **What's In A Name?** (Q 243). His choice, "Molly Brown," was eventually approved. However, the NASA Headquarters bureaucrats were so "ticked off" after the Grissom incident no spacecraft names were allowed for the remaining Gemini flights (4 through 12), nor for Apollo flights 7 and 8. For these missions, merely the official numerical designations were used. i.e. Gemini 4, 5 etc., through Gemini 12 and Apollo 7 and 8.

Beginning with Apollo 9, two spacecraft were flown for each Apollo mission and the crews were once again permitted to name them both. The CSM (Command and Service Module) accommodated all three crewmembers and the LM (Lunar Module) only had space for two (the crew to land on the Moon). Earlier in the program the designation LEM (Lunar Excursion Module) was used but it was shortened to LM (Lunar Module). The word, "excursion" seemed to suggest a holiday outing rather than the deadly serious business of landing on an extraterrestrial surface. However the acronym, LM, was still pronounced, "lem."

The Commander (CDR) and Lunar Module Pilot (LMP) would land on the Moon. The Command Module Pilot (CMP), who would orbit the Moon while his two crewmates landed, was given the privilege of naming the CSM. The CDR and LMP hashed out a name for the LM. It should be noted that during radio transmissions with the Mission Control Center the official mission designation was used as a call sign. e.g. "Apollo 9 this is Houston." The following are the crew-selected spacecraft names in the order they were flown.

1. Shepard	Mercury Redstone 3 (MR-3)	Freedom 7
2. Grissom	Mercury Redstone (MR-4)	Liberty Bell 7
3. Glenn	Mercury Atlas 6 (MA-6)	Friendship 7
4. Carpenter	Mercury Atlas (MA-7)	Aurora 7
5. Schirra	Mercury Atlas (MA-8)	Sigma 7
6. Cooper	Mercury Atlas (MA-9)	Faith 7
7. Grissom & Young	Gemini-Titan III (GT-3)	Molly Brown

Spacecraft for the following were not named: Gemini 4, 5, 6, 7, 8, 9, 10, 11 & 12; Apollo 7 & 8.

For entries 8 through 16 below, the crew names are given in the following order: CDR (Commander), CMP (Command Module Pilot), LMP (Lunar Module Pilot). Spacecraft engineering/manufacturing designations are not given.

8. McDivitt, Scott & Schweickart	Apollo 9	CSM: Gumdrop	LM: Spider
9. Stafford, Young & Cernan	Apollo 10	CSM: Charlie Brown	LM: Snoopy
10. Armstrong, Collins & Aldrin	Apollo 11	CSM: Columbia	LM: Eagle
11. Conrad, Gordon & Bean	Apollo 12	CSM: Yankee Clipper	LM: Intrepid
12. Lovell, Swigert & Haise	Apollo 13	CSM: Odyssey	LM: Aquarius
13. Shepard, Roosa & Mitchell	Apollo 14	CSM: Kitty Hawk	LM: Antares
14. Scott, Worden & Irwin	Apollo 15	CSM: Endeavour	LM: Falcon
15. Young, Mattingly & Duke	Apollo 16	CSM: Casper	LM: Orion
16. Cernan, Evans & Schmitt	Apollo 17	CSM: Challenger	LM: America

The name, Skylab, was selected for the program after a NASA-wide name submission contest. Skylab and Apollo-Soyuz spacecraft were not named. Official designation of Skylab missions were:

Skylab 1: Launch of the Skylab space station by a Saturn V.
Skylabs 2, 3 and 4 launched by Saturn 1B rockets for manned visits to Skylab.
The last launch of an Apollo-type spacecraft was the Apollo-Soyuz joint mission in 1975.

The Space Shuttle Orbiters' engineering/manufacturing designations are listed in addition to their names. The names were selected by NASA Headquarters (except for the Enterprise) with the following explanations regarding their names. OV is an abbreviation for Orbiter Vehicle.

Egr.No.	Name	Namesakes (All except the Enterprise were named for famous sailing ships.)
OV-101	Enterprise	Named after the fictional starship of the Star Trek television series. The Enterprise never flew in space. See Q. 231.
OV-102	Columbia	Named for a U.S. Navy sailing frigate that circumnavigated the globe. circa 1840.
OV-099	Challenger	Named for a U.S. Navy ship that made a prolonged exploration of the oceans (1872–76).
OV-103	Discovery	Named for two ships: British explorer Henry Hudson's ship (1610–11) used in an attempt to find a northwest passage from the Atlantic to the Pacific (through what is now Canada) and also after one of British Captain James Cook's ships used in exploring the Pacific ocean.

| OV-104 | Atlantis | Named after a two-masted ketch operated for the Woods Hole Oceanographic Institute from 1930 to 1966, which traveled more than half a million miles performing ocean research. |
| OV-105 | Endeavour | Also named after one of the ships commanded by Captain James Cook during exploration of the Pacific ocean. |

Note that the names, Columbia, Endeavour and Challenger are repeats of the names for the CSMs for Apollo 11, 15 and 17, respectively. Appendix A, above.

Appendix B: Lunar Landing Sites

Apollos 11, 12 and 14 landed very close to the equator; Apollos 15, 16 and 17 landed farther from the lunar equator to explore a greater variety of lunar topography. Fra Mauro was the site planned for Apollo 13 and was reassigned to Apollo 14 when Apollo 13 aborted the lunar landing.

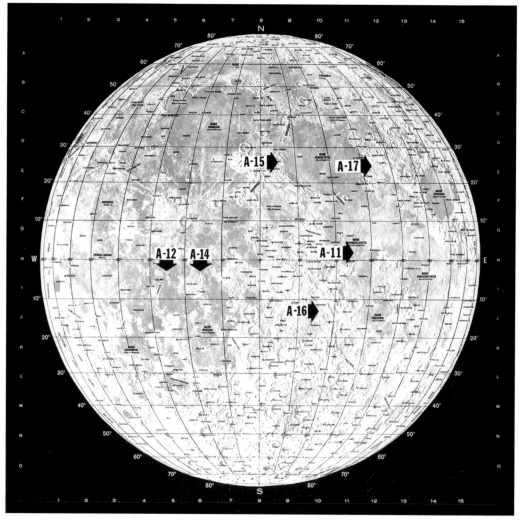

Illustration: A graphic depicting the lunar landing sites.

Mission	Landing Site Description	Approximate Lunar Coordinates of Landing
Apollo 11	Sea of Tranquility	0.67° North Latitude 23.47° East Longitude
Apollo 12	Ocean of Storms	3.01° South Latitude 23.42° West Longitude
Apollo 14	Fra Mauro Formation	3.64° South Latitude 17.45° West Longitude
Apollo 15	Hadley Apennines (Rille)	26.13° North Latitude 3.63° East Longitude
Apollo 16	Descartes highlands	8.98° South Latitude 15.50° East Longitude
Apollo 17	Taurus Littrow Valley	20.18° North Latitude 30.77° East Longitude

Appendix C: g-Forces

The standard measurement unit for describing forces which people feel from the Earth's gravity or during accelerated motion is called the "g". The lowercase "g" comes from the word, gravity. One "g" is the force you experience from the Earth's gravity at sea level. If you climbed Mt. Everest you would feel slightly less force (You would weigh less at 5½ miles above sea level).

Aside from catastrophic injuries resulting from falls (off a horse or off a cliff), people weren't exposed (routinely) to high acceleration forces until the development of motorized transportation. The airplane in particular subjected operators and passengers to unfamiliar forces generated during tight turns, loops and other aerobatic maneuvers as well as during inverted flight. Fliers measured the forces in the standard unit, "g." However, in addition to measuring the force as "so many g's", it became necessary to describe the direction of the force applied to the body during maneuvers.

They developed a colorful and highly descriptive method to convey the sense or direction of the force. If the force acted to force them harder down into the seat, the "g-forces" were said to be "eyeballs down." if the maneuver tended to lift them up and out of the seat, the force was called "eyeballs up." In the Apollo spacecraft, the crewmen lay on their backs during launch and, when the booster approached staging, the crewmembers were pressed harder and harder back into their couches at about four times their Earth weight. This was called 4 g's, "eyeballs in", because the force tended to force their eyeballs back into their heads. When the engines shut down suddenly (at staging), the astronauts were thrust forward into their restraining straps and felt an "eyeballs out" force for a fraction of a second.

"Eyeballs down" acceleration is also called a positive g-force, or pulling "positive g's." To generate this force in an aircraft, the pilot has to pull back on the control stick (column yoke or side hand controller). Conversely, "Eyeballs up" acceleration is called a negative g-force. Most pilots also refer to this as pulling "negative g's", even though it takes a push force on the control stick.

The terms positive and negative came into common use when fighter aircraft had a "g-meter" installed on the instrument panel. When you flew right side up in level flight the needle of the meter read one-g (positive); if you did a simple loop the meter might read "three-g's (positive) in the tightest part of the maneuver. If you flew upside down in level flight, the meter read one-g (negative). The needle went up and was labeled + (positive) for eyeballs down flight. The needle moved down and was labeled with a minus sign "-" (negative) for eyeballs up flight. Halfway between +1 and -1 was "0" (zero). If a pilot flew the aircraft in a "nose-over" maneuver so that the needle read "0", then the pilot was at zero-g. In other words the pilot was weightless as long as the needle read "zero" hence the term, zero-g.

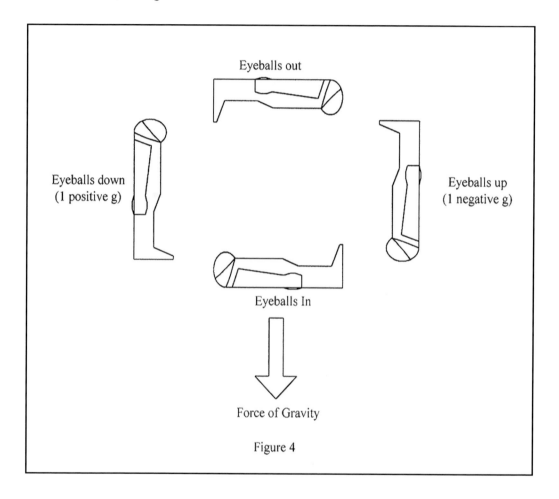

Figure 4

Look for these other important books about space flight at your local retailer!

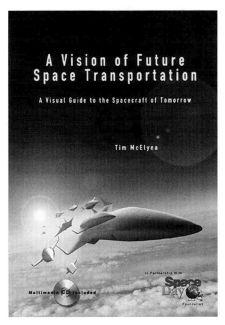

**$25.95 USA $34.95 CDN £21.95 UK
ISBN 1-896522-93-9**

A Vision Of Future Space Transportation
by Tim McElyea

The glorious space age has come and gone. So what now? What's next? To go further, to go faster, we must take the next step. Space is still full of mystery and challenges humankind as much as ever. Ideas on what the next step, or steps are vary greatly and there is no shortage of concepts for the future of space transportation. Concepts include new engines, new strategies, harnessing gravity, electromagnetism, nuclear and more. This book will take you on a guided visual tour of the future of space transportation. From Earth to Orbit to In-Space transportation, you will sample what is being considered and get an easy-to-understand explanation of what the spacecraft will do and how it will work. This book is the culmination of years of work with NASA and hours of interviews with leading propulsion scientists and aerospace innovators. Decades ago Dr. Wernher von Braun teamed with Walt Disney to animate a mission to Mars and inspired a generation. Today multimedia, animation and video serve a similar communication need. The CD-ROM included contains official NASA videos, vehicle concept animation, and dynamic multimedia. View spacecraft concepts in 3D, see mission animation and hear first hand what the visionaries of the aerospace industry hope to accomplish.

* Includes Bonus CD-ROM

**$28.95 USA $39.95 CDN £25.95 UK
ISBN 1-896522-88-2**

Lost Spacecraft
The Search For Liberty Bell 7

by Curt Newport

introduction by Tom Hanks

Lost Spacecraft: The Search for Liberty Bell 7, describes the exploration of two unique and dangerous environments, space and underwater, and how the paths of two men, one living and one dead, crossed in the recovery of the Liberty Bell-7 spacecraft. Lost Spacecraft focuses on two periods, one beginning in 1959, the other in 1985, interweaving the stories of Project Mercury, Gus Grissom and his ill-fated Mercury flight, on-going developments in deep ocean exploration, and Curt Newport's 14 year obsession to raise the sunken space-age Titanic from the depths of the Atlantic Ocean. Also told is how Newport's team, against staggering odds, managed to find the phone-booth sized space vehicle during his harrowing 1999 expedition, only to see their recovery vehicle and Liberty Bell 7 ripped from their grasp by the forces of nature. Newport later recovered Liberty Bell 7 during what remains the deepest commercial salvage operation in history, returning Grissom's craft to Cape Canaveral, Florida thirty-eight years to the day after Grissom blasted off his tiny launch pad. However, the prevalent theme running through Lost Spacecraft is how simple luck almost rivals technical ability when exploring any deadly environment, whether it be the silent void of low-Earth orbit, or the crushing cold of the abyss.

* Includes Bonus CD-ROM

VIRTUAL APOLLO
A Pictorial Essay of the Engineering and Construction of the Apollo Command and Service Modules
by Scott P. Sullivan

With this book, for the first time the public can become acquainted with the Apollo spacecraft in detail and learn the story of its design and construction. Full color drawings in exacting detail provide inside and out views of the Command and Service Modules complete with details of construction and fabrication. The Apollo spacecraft is the most intricate and exacting machine ever built, and it had to be as near to perfect as it could be made, every time. With over 3 million components, a performance record of 99.9% would still leave 3,000 parts that could fail -- any one of which might result in the deaths of the crew. With the exception of Apollo 13, the spacecraft lived up to expectations on every lunar mission, and even Apollo 13, after a major explosion, managed to circle the Moon and bring its crew home safely. Virtual Apollo is a book long overdue; the care and completeness with which it has been created speak for themselves. Thanks to the dedication and hard work that have gone into this book, we can now truly appreciate the magnificent machine that was the Apollo spacecraft and marvel at the achievements of the many thousands of engineers and technicians who stayed on Earth but were on the mission every step of the way.

$17.95 USA $24.95 CDN £14.95 UK
ISBN 1-896522-94-7

APOLLO EECOM
Journey of a Lifetime
by Sy Liebergot with David M. Harland

Most of what we learn about NASA's space missions comes from statements carefully planned and massaged by managers and public relations people. With Apollo EECOM: Journey of a Lifetime we finally get an insider's view of how the Flight Controllers operated and just what they faced when events were crucial. This book is the life story of Sy Liebergot, former NASA Flight Controller, with emphasis on his years working in Mission Control. Following the disastrous tank explosion during the Apollo 13 mission, it was the Flight Controllers that made possible the safe return of the three endangered astronauts. Aboard Apollo 13, Lovell, Haise and Swigert performed wonders battling for their lives, but without the expertise, quick thinking and technical support of Mission Control, they never could have come home. Sy Liebergot was there and relates the details as they really happened. And Apollo 13 is just one of the many exciting stories he tells us. Truly and insider's view, this book discusses not just the events, but also the people that decided and enacted those events. These are the details that were never shown on anyone's TV screen; finally we get to learn what type of people the NASA Mission Controllers really were, and how they handled the demanding tasks that were theirs alone.

$26.95 USA $37.95 CDN £23.95 UK
ISBN 1-896522-96-3

* Includes CD-ROM

THE ROCKET TEAM

by Frederick I. Ordway III
Mitchell Sharpe

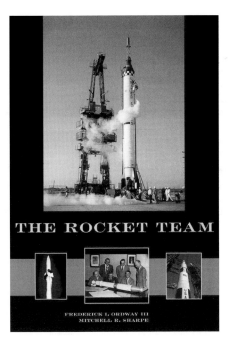

Traveling to the Moon and the planets beyond has moved from the world of dreamers and Buck Rogers to the factual terrain of the daily papers and television news shows. This book tells the story of the men who did so much to make the impossible a reality. From a small group of amateur rocketeers led by Wernher von Braun, his rocket team grew into one of the most influential technological forces in this or any other century. The Rocket Team discloses much previously classified information, particularly involving the British intelligence effort to learn about Hitler's heralded V1 and V2 "vengeance weapons"; to delay their going into action and to minimize their effec-tiveness once they were developed. The U.S. and British documents, as well as information from von Braun himself, his papers, and interviews with the other members of his team, provide new insights into the wartime growth of rocketry.

FREDERICK I. ORDWAY III worked with Wernher von Braun at the former Army Ballistic Missile Agency and later at the NASA-Marshall Space Flight Center in Huntsville, Ala. He is a member of many leading professional societies and is the au-thor, co-author, or editor of more than thirty books and over two hundred articles. MITCHELL R. SHARPE has been closely identified with the national space program for more than twenty years and is the au-thor of several books on space flight.

Includes Bonus disc with videos & images
ISBN 1-894959-00-0

INTERSTELLAR TRAVEL

Written by top members of the American Association for the Advancement of Science
Edited by Yoji Kondo, Frederick C. Bruhweiler, John Moore and Charles Sheffield

Instead of blindly following popular preconceptions and biases about matters that we have not yet had the chance to test or verify, examined in this volume is our current state of knowledge, as well as our present state of ignorance, on subjects related to interstellar travel. The science and technology of the future that would be available for building interstellar space ships would indeed be quite different from those imagined from the perspectives of the early twenty-first century. Nevertheless, it is a good idea to start thinking what it will take to mount such an undertaking so that we can begin exploring various scientific and engineering possibilities now -- rather than wait endlessly for 'the right time' to come.

$21.95 USA $29.95 CDN £18.95 UK
ISBN 1-896522-99-8

1. Contents
2. Dedication - The dedication to Sheffield and Bob Forward.
3. Preface - Preface by the Editors
4. Overview by Y. Kondo
5. "Fly Me to the Stars' by Sheffield
6. Acknowledgements
7. "the Ultimate Exploration.." by G. Landis
8. "Colonizing Other Worlds" by J. Haldeman
9. "Why we must go" by D. Beason
10. "Kin-based Crews.." by J. Moore
11. figure for article by Moore (in Powerpoint)
12. "Genetic Considerations..." by D. O'Rourke
13. Glossary for O'Rourke article.
14. "language Change..." by S. Thomason
15. "Looking for Life.." by F. Dyson
16. "Remembering Charles Sheffield " by Y. Kondo
17. "Reminiscences: Bob Forward" by Landis
18. Untitled Contribution by Bob Forward

Apogee Books Space Series

TITLE	ISBN #	$ US	$ CDN	£ UK
Freedom 7 The NASA Mission Reports	1-896522-80-7	16.95	23.95	15.95
Frienship 7 The NASA Mission Reports	1-896522-60-2	16.95	23.95	11.95
Sigma 7 The NASA Mission Reports	1-894959-01-9	19.95	27.95	16.95
Gemini 6 The NASA Mission Reports	1-896522-61-0	16.95	23.95	13.95
Gemini 7 The NASA Mission Reports	1-896522-82-3	17.95	24.95	15.95
Apollo 7 The NASA Mission Reports	1-896522-64-5	16.95	23.95	13.95
Apollo 8 The NASA Mission Reports 2nd Edition	1-896522-66-1	16.95	23.95	13.95
Apollo 9 The NASA Mission Reports	1-896522-51-3	14.95	20.95	9.95
Apollo 10 The NASA Mission Reports 2nd Edition	1-896522-68-8	16.95	23.95	13.95
Apollo 11 The NASA Mission Reports Volume One	1-896522-53-X	16.95	23.95	13.95
Apollo 11 The NASA Mission Reports Volume Two	1-896522-49-1	13.95	18.95	10.95
Apollo 11 The NASA Mission Reports Volume Three	1-896522-85-8	24.95	34.95	19.95
Apollo 12 The NASA Mission Reports	1-896522-54-8	16.95	23.95	13.95
Apollo 13 The NASA Mission Reports	1-896522-55-6	16.95	23.95	13.95
Apollo 14 The NASA Mission Reports	1-896522-56-4	16.95	23.95	15.95
Apollo 15 The NASA Mission Reports Volume One	1-896522-57-2	17.95	24.95	15.95
Apollo 16 The NASA Mission Reports Volume One	1-896522-58-0	19.95	27.95	15.95
Apollo 17 The NASA Mission Reports Volume One	1-896522-59-9	19.95	27.95	15.95
X - 15 The NASA Mission Reports	1-896522-65-3	21.95	29.95	18.95
STS 1-5 The NASA Mission Reports	1-896522-69-6	21.95	29.95	18.95
MARS The NASA Mission Reports	1-896522-62-9	21.95	29.95	15.95
Rocket And Space Corporation Energia	1-896522-81-5	19.95	28.95	16.95
Arrows To The Moon	1-896522-83-1	19.95	28.95	17.95
The High Frontier - Human Colonies In Space	1-896522-67-X	19.95	28.95	17.95
The Unbroken Chain	1-896522-84-X	26.95	37.95	24.95
Creating Space - The Story of the Space Age Through Models	1-896522-86-6	29.95	39.95	24.95
Woman Astronauts	1-896522-87-4	21.95	29.95	18.95
On To Mars- Colonising A New World	1-896522-90-4	19.95	27.95	16.95
The Conquest Of Space	1-896522-92-0	21.95	30.95	19.95
Lost Spacecraft - The Search For Liberty Bell 7	1-896522-88-2	28.95	39.95	25.95
Virtual Apollo	1-896522-94-7	17.95	24.95	14.95
Apollo EECOM - Journey Of A Lifetime	1-896522-96-3	25.95	36.95	22.95
DYNA-SOAR - Hypersonic Strategic Weapons System	1-896522-95-5	29.95	39.95	24.95
Interstellar Travel & Multi-Generational Spacecraft	1-896522-99-8	19.95	28.95	17.95
Space Trivia	1-896522-98-X	17.95	24.95	14.95
The Rocket Team	1-894959-00-0	TBA	TBA	TBA
WOMEN OF SPACE: Cool Careers On The Final Frontier	1-894959-03-5	24.95	34.95	19.95
A Vision Of Future Space Transportation	1-896522-93-9	25.95	34.95	21.95

www.apogeespacebooks.com